"Russell Targ's *Third Eye Spies* is a masterwork in the history and practice of remote viewing. I can sympathize with those who find it difficult to believe that our awareness can transcend the everyday limits of space and time. It sounds like a fantasy. But having known and worked directly with many of the people mentioned in this book, I know firsthand that what Targ describes in this book is both true and accurate. I recommend *Third Eye Spies* to anyone interested in learning about the modern rediscovery of a fascinating human ability."

—**Dean Radin,** MS, PhD, chief scientist at the
Institute of Noetic Sciences and author of
Real Magic and other books

"*Third Eye Spies* was written by Russell Targ, who is a gem and a noted expert in exploring expanding levels of consciousness. In this fascinating book, he shares with readers how some of the most gifted remote viewers of our time use their intuition. I love the photos and diagrams of how remote viewing works, so readers can get a hands-on feel for ways to use it in their own lives. Highly recommended for everyone who wants to develop their intuitive gifts."

—**Judith Orloff,** MD, psychiatrist and
New York Times bestselling author of *Second Sight*

"Russell provides friendly and—more importantly—easy guidance for people who have never tried remote viewing before and want to take their first steps."

—**Paul H. Smith,** PhD (Major, US Army, ret.)

"Russell Targ is one of the small group who successfully demonstrated remote viewing and is one of its masters. If you are interested in remote viewing, you should pay close attention to anything he has to say on the subject."

—**Stephan A. Schwartz,** au

"Remote viewing has been the most exciting development in parapsychology in my own and my colleagues' work in the last fifty years. It's not just intellectually exciting, it has often been a practical application of ESP helping real intelligence agencies like the CIA gather information that wasn't available otherwise. When people ask me where to go for accurate, serious, and fascinating reading about remote viewing, Russell Targ's books, such as *Third Eye Spies*, are always at the top of my recommendations list."

—**Charles Tart,** professor, University of California, Davis, and author of *States of Consciousness* and *Open Mind, Discriminating Mind*

"Using simple language and just enough facts and stories so the reader knows this is the real deal, Russell tells the story of how he found the path to his destiny despite not being able to see the yellow brick road under his feet! But Russell also talks of time and casualty, using the clear language of laser physics which he pursued for thirty years. As Russell says, there is no separation between out-of-body experiences and remote viewing, just a long hallway of possibilities, ready and waiting for someone to try it out. Russell's book gives me a picture of how to do it."

—**David Gladstone,** San Francisco historian

Third Eye Spies

THIRD EYE SPIES

Learn Remote Viewing from the Masters

RUSSELL TARG

Foreword by Paul H. Smith, PhD

NEW
PAGE

This edition first published in 2023 by New Page Books, an imprint of
Red Wheel/Weiser, LLC
With offices at:
65 Parker Street, Suite 7
Newburyport, MA 01950
www.redwheelweiser.com

Copyright © 2023 by Russell Targ
Foreword © 2023 by Paul H. Smith

ISBN: 978-1-63748-013-7
Library of Congress Cataloging-in-Publication Data available upon
request.

Cover design by Sky Peck Design
Photo of Chicago elevated train on page 63 by Shutterstock; Eileen Garrett
book cover on page 114, used by permission of Lisette Coly; Wall Street
Journal reproduction on page 124, used by permission; image of Padma-
sambhava on page 129 by Shutterstock; all other photos/images courtesy
of Russell Targ
Interior by Timm Bryson, em em design, LLC
Typeset in Minion Pro

Printed in the United States of America
IBI
10 9 8 7 6 5 4 3 2 1

FOR PATTY,
with all my love and heartfelt gratitude for her love, support, and encouragement through this and all my writing—and the other mishegoss of my eighty-eighth year.

AND FOR:
Albert Einstein, Boris Podolsky, and Nathan Rosen, who were the first courageous physicists to point out to us that quantum theory requires entanglement and "spooky action at a distance."

"Psi" is not a set of special categories defined by telepathy, clairvoyance, OOB, and precognition, but rather it is a broad spectrum of capabilities—"super faculties"—latent in us all. These capabilities give rise to our unlimited human potential.

—INGO SWANN

CONTENTS

Contents

ILLUSTRATIONS AND TABLES

Acknowledgements

It is my pleasure to thank my dear friend, Judy Chadderdon, without whose help through hours on the phone, this book would not exist. She found thoughtful and imaginative ways to turn my collection of chapter outlines into something that a publisher might consider worth publishing. Thank you with all my heart.

I also want to thank my longtime friend and colleague, Stephan Schwartz, for contributing his thoughtful remembrances of his interactions with our great psychics and friends Ingo Swann and Hella Hammid.

I would like to sincerely thank Dr. Jeffrey Mishlove for his many thoughtful interviews of me during this past year. These searching interviews stimulated me to gather all my notes to write what has turned out to be my personal history of teaching remote viewing.

Above all, I want to express my deep appreciation to Hella Hammid, Pat Price, Ingo Swann, Joe McMoneagle, and Gary Langford, who all generously contributed their powerful and unique psychic gifts to the successful outcome of our research.

And finally, I want to thank Lance Mungia, who was the director, and coproducer with me, of the 2018 documentary film, *Third Eye Spies*, which was the inspiration for this book.

FOREWORD

I was an Army psychic spy. Yes, really! For the military. A *psychic spy*. For nearly all of the seven years that I was a captain in the US Army, I was first trained and then used my extrasensory perceptual (ESP) abilities to project my consciousness to locations both foreign and domestic. These were abilities I never even knew I had before I was recruited to learn how to use them. Specifically, I am talking about what is known as "remote viewing," or "RV" for short.

As Russell notes early in this book, the term "remote viewing" was coined by legendary New York artist and parapsychologist Ingo Swann. (Full disclosure: Swann taught me remote viewing, and I will be ever grateful, both to him and to the taxpayers who funded it.)

To be succinct: remote viewing is a skill that capitalizes on an aspect of consciousness we all possess. We have it simply by virtue of being human, and it allows us to experience, perceive, and describe people, places, and things that are hidden from us by distance, shielding, or even the past or (to some degree) the future. I often refer to this skill as a form of "disciplined clairvoyance."

I was one of several military officers, enlisted soldiers, and government civilians who were taught to use this form of "disciplined clairvoyance" to spy out Soviet research facilities, advanced weapons, and scientific laboratories. We "looked" for hostages taken by Hezbollah in Lebanon, hunted narcotics traffickers off America's coasts, "observed" Chinese nuclear tests, "invaded" the Kremlin, and dug into emerging defense technology—both ours and the "other guy's."

There were times, of course, when this psychic skill didn't work. On the other hand, there were many occasions when it *absolutely* worked—sometimes spectacularly. (Similar impressive results are presented in this book.) Given that skeptics laugh at the idea that ESP should *ever* work, the amount of concrete evidence we developed left us laughing last and best.

In large measure, I owe my career as a psychic spy to the author of this book, Russell Targ. Russ, along with his colleagues at the highly regarded California think tank SRI International had the courage to swim upstream against the tide of orthodox science. Their task was to fill a hole in our defenses that the US intelligence community could not itself plug. If they had not so successfully plugged that hole, I never would have had the opportunity to become a psychic spy.

In the 1960s and early 1970s, the Central Intelligence Agency fretted about massive Soviet military spending in fields that Western "experts" generally dismissed as "paranormal." (To them, "paranormal" is a synonym for "fantasy.") This worry led the CIA to physicist Hal Puthoff's laboratory door at SRI in the fall of 1972. The agents gave him a check for $50,000 as seed money and asked him to set up a program investigating the kinds of paranormal phenomena on which the Soviets already had a head start.

Russell, who had a long-standing interest in these topics, had recently become acquainted with Hal and, now that there was an actual "program" to join, he was invited to SRI to partner with Hal in creating what ultimately evolved into the Star Gate psychic spy program. Star Gate was run by the US government for the next twenty-three years, ending only with the conclusion of the Cold War. Thus history was made.

My task here is to briefly introduce you to this marvelous book, clarify the context, and set the stage for what follows.

When journalists write about the "CIA Star Gate Program," they often start off confused, and it just gets worse from there. They think that because the Program has a singular name, it must have had a monolithic structure. But that is wrong. The first point to make is that the program only was called Star Gate late in its existence. Before that it was known under a variety of arcane titles, such as Scanate, Grill Flame, and Sun Streak, to name a few. The Star Gate moniker stuck because it was the last name by which the program was known.

It's best if you think of Star Gate as two parallel, yet connected efforts—two forking trunks of the same tree, if you will. The first trunk was Star Gate's research arm, created to investigate psychic phenomena, specifically remote viewing. Begun and home-based at SRI and helmed by Russell and Hal, this effort was funded under contract initially by the CIA and served as the foundation from which everything else developed.

After the CIA was forced to abandon the SRI program in 1975, the source of money and guidance switched to various

Department of Defense (DoD) activities, starting with the Air Force, then the Army, and finally the Defense Intelligence Agency (DIA). (Russell often mentions his great respect for Lieutenant General James Williams, under whom the long-standing relationship between DIA and remote viewing began.)

Ironically, the CIA never again "ran" the Star Gate Program. Though Star Gate is widely called the CIA's program, the agency's only additional role was to do away with it in June 1995. To those of us with ties to Star Gate, this was much like giving the beloved dog that you can no longer care for to a trusted neighbor, whose first act on taking ownership was to shoot it. Hard feelings? Yeah, maybe some.

Once established, the SRI effort (later moved to Science Applications International Corporation, or SAIC, under Dr. Ed May) was to make its findings available to its customer, the DoD, for use in the other branch of Star Gate, the military "psychic spy" unit. Some operational (that is, practical) work was done at SRI, but the majority of what Russell and his colleagues did there was scientific. It is largely those results and his experiences in helping generate them that Russ mines for our benefit in this book.

After a sojourn at Wright-Patterson Air Force Base under Air Force civilian analyst Dale Graff, the military branch of Star Gate came to rest at Fort George G. Meade, Maryland, in the late 1970s. It lived its life there through several incarnations (I won't bore you with the bureaucratic details).

First administered by the Army's Intelligence and Security Command, administrative ownership of the unit was passed to DIA headquarters at Bolling Air Force Base, District of

Columbia, at the start of 1986, though the actual remote view-ers stayed at Ft. Meade.

We Star Gate viewers performed over 2,500 intelligence collection missions for two dozen intelligence community and military agencies. Just some of the list includes the National Security Agency, the Joint Chiefs of Staff, the US Secret Service, the DEA, US Forces Korea, the Army's Intelligence Threat and Analysis Center, and the National Security Council. Our most prolific requestor, ironically, was the organization that in the end shut Star Gate down—the Central Intelligence Agency.

Until Congress transferred Star Gate to the CIA (leading, as mentioned, to the program's immediate demise), the DIA directed and funded the research at SRI (and later SAIC). This research significantly advanced remote viewing and other consciousness science. The world owes Russell and his col-leagues a debt of gratitude for the profound insights from which we all may benefit.

Russell, though, had his own plans. Seeking a more relaxed climate for consciousness research than the often stifling clas-sified security envelope government contracts demand, Russell left after ten years at SRI in 1982 and branched out into other activities. He has never looked back.

In my talks with him about this project, Russell often calls this a "remote viewing picture-book." Director/producer Lance Mungia's successful documentary film *Third Eye Spies*, in which Russ plays the central role, gave Russ the idea for a companion book. And this book, itself now appropriately titled *Third Eye Spies*, serves as a canvass on which to assem-ble and add to the vignettes and interviews that emerged in the film.

Gathered here are remote viewing stories and images, some never before published, all brought together in a form more accessible than film can sometimes be. After all, even if the power is out, we can still pick up a book from the shelf anytime we want to refresh our memory or remind ourselves of something we loved in it. Try doing the same with a film.

Perhaps some of the most fascinating parts of *Third Eye Spies* (the book) are the chapters on precognition (in other words, "seeing" events or getting information from the future) and on how to actually launch a basic remote viewing experience for yourself. The latter is particularly helpful. Many folks want to try this skill, but have no idea where to begin. Russell provides friendly and—more importantly—easy guidance for people who have never tried remote viewing before and want to take their first steps. He gives you the basic secrets that he has successfully used over and over again in his many live workshops and appearances to help folks from Italian housewives to American businesspeople have their first empowering remote viewing experiences.

Russell now finds himself on the long end of life. One senses in him the urge many of us feel, once we realize we have unexpectedly become "chronologically challenged" by age, to document important things that didn't quite fit together in past tellings of our histories. This book is memorable for many reasons, and I invite you to give it the chance it deserves.

Paul H. Smith, PhD (Major, US Army, ret.)
Cedar City, Utah
April 2022

INTRODUCTION

I have been successfully teaching people how to get in touch with their psychic abilities for more than fifty years. This began in 1972 when I co-founded an extrasensory perception (ESP) research program at Stanford Research Institute. It was funded by the Central Intelligence Agency (CIA). We performed many fascinating double-blind experiments for the CIA, with very successful results. Among these, we described a hidden Russian weapons factory in Siberia and a failed Chinese atomic bomb test, located a downed Russian bomber in Africa, and located several kidnapped US officials. One was the ambassador to Iran during the Iran hostage crisis. Another was an American general kidnapped in Italy by the Red Brigades radical terrorist group. Early in the program, we even identified the ringleader of the Patty Hearst kidnapping, for which we received a commendation from the Berkeley Police Department.

This program was so successful that in 1978 the United States Army invited us to train six Army intelligence officers to create an Army psychic corps known as Project Star Gate. Star Gate provided useful secret and top-secret information to the military until 1995. One of my purposes here is to correct the misconception that psi, a more modern term for ESP, is weak and unreliable. On the contrary, in our laboratory experiments and classified operational tasks, psi was found to be surprisingly reliable, accurate, and useful. In this book, I will introduce you to the most successful and gifted remote viewers who participated in our program, many of whom had never done any psi-oriented work like this before.

Remote viewing is the ability to mentally experience and describe distant or unseen people, places, events, and objects from the past or present or future. The proof for ESP is so strong it would be statistically unreasonable to deny it. In data from laboratories all over the world, we see that the accuracy and reliability of remote viewing is not in any way degraded by distance. It is no more difficult to describe Soviet Siberia than it is to describe a park across the street. Similarly, it is no harder to describe an event hours or days in the future, than it is to describe a present-time event. For example, we were able to successfully forecast changes in the silver commodity market nine times in a row, earning us and our investor a quarter million dollars. So, the future can be known.

The world around us may look finite, but fifty years of research into psychic abilities and verified out-of-body experiences have convinced me that our awareness is *limitless in space and time*, and therefore we are also limitless. This is the basic finding from our two decades of remote viewing research at Stanford Research Institute (SRI). Through my work in this area, I have taught thousands of people all over the world how to get in touch with the part of themselves that is psychic. I hope this remote viewing "picture book" will help you do the same.

Remote viewing teaches that you are not just a physical body—not just meat and potatoes. Who we are is indestructible, timeless awareness and not what you see in the morning mirror. If you think that who you are is what you see in the mirror, then you are in for a lot of unnecessary suffering. I would say that the meaning of life is to experience our primordial timeless awareness and to teach that. *I hope to give you an experience of that in this book.*

CHAPTER 1

Ingo Swann: The Father of Remote Viewing

Figure 1. Ingo Swann, artist and psychic

Our total psychic range is quite astonishing. It is fabulous beyond what most people can conceive.

—INGO SWANN

I ngo Swann was a life-long psychic practitioner and the father of remote viewing at Stanford Research Institute (SRI). He was a visionary artist from New York, who taught us how to separate the psychic signal from the mental noise in order to receive information. Mental noise, or analytical overlay (AOL) as Ingo Swann called it, is the confusion caused by naming or grasping at your mental images. Although an initial flash of AOL might well contain bits of valuable correct information, it may be partially concealed by the analytic noise.

An example of this is illustrated by one of our inexperienced remote viewers, who put her own meaning on what she psychically saw. Rather than just describing what she was experiencing, she said, "I know where he is. He is in Macy's department store." I said, "That doesn't really sound like remote viewing. Can you tell me what you are experiencing that makes you say Macy's?" The remote viewer then said, "I see something that looks like a bunch of coat hangers all in a row, hanging on a rod." I then asked the viewer to draw what she was experiencing. She drew coat hangers all in a row, which greatly resembled the actual target, which was a pedestrian overpass (see Figure 19 on page 33).

This source of mental noise was first identified by the Buddhist dharma master Padmasambhava in his book *Self-Liberation through Seeing with Naked Awareness*, written in approximately 800 AD after he moved from India to Tibet. Ingo Swann followed up 1,200 years later and taught the very important idea that *naming, guessing, grasping, memory, analysis,* and *imagination* are all sources of mental noise that interfere with your ability to receive a psychic signal and experience the remote viewing target. Guessing the target and naming the target are the worst among them. Ingo told us about the importance of the elements of the "psychic triad, which must all work together in a balanced and harmonious fashion. These are *intellect, feeling/emotion sensing, and intuition*. These elements can lead the student on the path of psychic revelation."[1]

Padmasambhava taught that we should seek unconditioned timeless awareness instead of conditioned awareness. By which we mean moving from the conditioned awareness of self-centered ego-based craving and fear into unconditioned spacious awareness and freedom. Remote viewing can be considered a kind of timeless awareness. There is no dogma associated with it. You just take a couple of deep breaths, close your eyes, and observe the surprising images that show up in your awareness. Since your nature is timeless, your awareness is not limited by cause and effect.

Ingo showed us this temporal freedom in his remote viewing when he was asked by two CIA operatives who came to our lab to discover what would occur at a given set of geographical coordinates three days in the future. Ingo quieted his mind, then said he needed colored pencils to draw the pyrotechnic display he was psychically watching. He said, "I see beautiful bright streamers rising into the sky, and a line of trucks in the background. It's like the Fourth of July." From his description, the CIA could tell that he was describing a failed atomic bomb test. No mushroom cloud, just uranium burning in the sky. This valuable information was confirmed to us three days later by the CIA contractors who monitored our program.

In a pivotal incident during our program, on May 29, 1973, Ingo Swann remotely viewed a top-secret National Security Agency (NSA) facility in Sugar Grove, West Virginia. It served as a secret government listening post for Soviet satellite communications. According to the *New York Times*, at the time

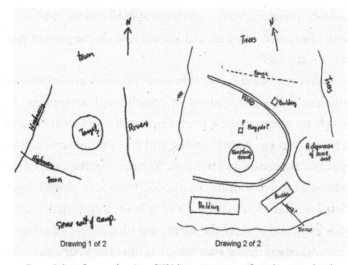

Figure 2. Ingo Swann, drawing of NSA listening post, confirmed in every detail

of our experiment, Sugar Grove intercepted and processed almost all international communications entering the Eastern United States.

Dr. Kit Green, a CIA analyst who was interested in our work and served as one of our contract monitors, gave us a set of geographic coordinates for a remote viewing experiment. The target was a log cabin in the woods. Coincidentally, the cabin coordinates happened to be nearby the secret NSA facility. Rather than psychically perceiving the log cabin, which was the intended target, Ingo said, "I see rolling hills, a lawn, and a flag pole. There are old bunkers around, like an underground reservoir. This could be some kind of military base." Ingo then drew a large round building at the location, along with what turned out to be a large round microwave radar antenna, which was the actual function of the facility. Both Ingo and Pat Price, another remote viewer at SRI who participated that day, clairvoyantly zeroed in on the secret site rather than the log cabin.

Ingo used the images that showed up in his awareness to draw the secret Sugar Grove facility location and layout. Pat Price, on the other hand, experienced his awareness differently by flying over the site at 1,500 feet. He used mental imagery to find his way down into a basement workroom, where he psychically opened drawers of a filing cabinet and read several top-secret operational files with code words on them. The code words had a theme that pertained to the game of pool: "cue ball," "eight ball," "four ball," "eighteen ball," and "rack up" were written on the folders.[2]

On top of a desk were additional files. They were green. They had the code words "fly trap" and "minerva" written on them. These were part of a Special Access Program also classified as top secret. Even the classified name of the entire site had been located. It was called "hay fork." These files and words were subsequently confirmed by the CIA and NSA to be currently operational code words, meaning that they were in use at the time. In my film *Third Eye Spies*, CIA agents Kit Green and Ken Kress are seen in direct conversation, verifying that the Special Access code words remotely viewed at SRI were correct.

Our breach of this facility caused quite a stir. The NSA, furious about the breach, immediately confronted the CIA. They were angry that the Central Intelligence Agency appeared to be encouraging California psychics to spy on their most secret facility. Three days later, both agencies sent personnel to SRI to find out how our remote viewers accessed the Special Access files. I have been asked many times, "If a remote viewer can

Figure 3. Sugar Grove, NSA listening post, with microwave radar antennas

read top-secret code words in a basement safe, then couldn't he just as easily read the nuclear launch codes in the president's pocket?" Indeed, the intelligence community was fearful of that throughout our entire program.

As it turned out, our great success at Sugar Grove was the key to getting our first contract with the CIA. They funded us for the next twenty-two years. Wanting to know how such a feat was accomplished, the NSA official at the time asked Pat why he, like Ingo, had described the radar site instead of the intended log cabin, whose coordinates he was given. Pat said simply, "The more attention you place on hiding something, the more it shines like a beacon in psychic space."

After Sugar Grove, Ingo performed another remote viewing trial where he was given only geographic coordinates.

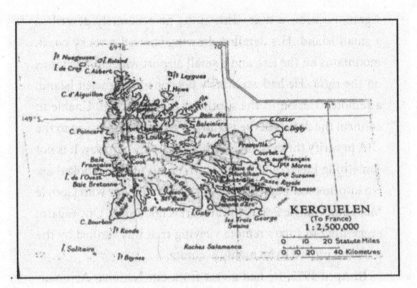

Figure 4a. National Geographic map of Kerguelen Island

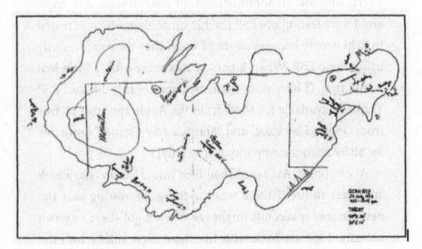

Figure 4b. Ingo Swann's psychic drawing of Kerguelen Island

Again, he drew a map. This time, he accurately described a small island. His detailed drawing showed a rocky coast, mountains on the left, and a small airport with storage tanks on the right. He had accurately described Kerguelen Island, a remote location in the southern Indian Ocean. Unable to confirm the details of the island ourselves, we had to go to the CIA to verify the existence of the airport and runway. It is not something Ingo could have known on his own nor looked up. No information was available to him. Even today with Google Maps and Google Earth, the airport is not visible. Once again, everything in Ingo's remote viewing trial was verified by the CIA and proved to be highly accurate.

In April 1973, we had a visit from our National Aeronautics and Space Administration (NASA) contract monitor, Art Reetz, who was an administrator for new projects. Art, Ingo, and I were testing my ESP teaching machine, which I created to help people become aware of when they were successfully using their ESP. When a person was successful, a little bell would ring. (I have since made two apps of this device: "ESP Trainer" [available for $0.99 from the Apple app store or free from Google Play store] and "Stargate ESP Trainer" [available for $0.99 from the Apple app store only].)

At one point, Art asked Ingo if he would like to take a look at Jupiter to see if there was anything interesting that the new Pioneer spacecraft might see when it got there in seven months. Ingo sat back with his cigar, blew smoke into the room, and asked for a clipboard and pen. He then described and drew a previously unknown ring of ice crystals around Jupiter, which was 500 million miles away. Art asked him if he wasn't thinking of Saturn. Ingo said to Art, "I have been

Figure 5. Modern ESP trainer app

looking at the solar system for my entire life, and I am well aware of the difference between Jupiter and Saturn."

The illustration on the next page is from the NASA Pioneer spacecraft that arrived at Jupiter seven months later, showing the newly discovered rings and ice crystals just as Ingo described them.

My good friend Stephan Schwartz, also a remote viewing researcher, worked with Ingo Swann and our great friend and psychic Hella Hammid for more than a decade. (More on Hella in chapter 4.) Stephan generously offered to contribute a couple of paragraphs to this book from his memories of these amazing, open-hearted psychics. Here he talks about Ingo:

"A few days before we were scheduled to do the Deep Quest study (remote viewing study of the Santa Catalina Channel), the two remote viewers I was going to work with suddenly were unable to participate. The great psychic Alan Vaughan

Figure 6a. NASA illustration of Jupiter with the newly found rings

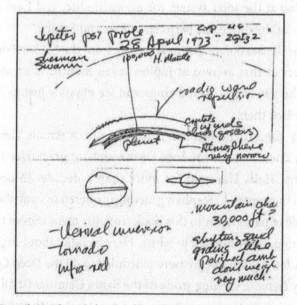

Figure 6b. Ingo Swann's drawing of Jupiter with its rings, seven months earlier

contracted a bad flu, and George McMullen, also an experienced remote viewer, had a co-worker at the Chrysler dealership where he worked suddenly take time off and George had to cover for him. At the last minute, I was introduced to Ingo Swann by physicist Ed May at SRI. He, Ed, and Hal Puthoff, who were all Scientologists at the time, came down to the Scientology Celebrity Center in Hollywood, California, to meet me. I had heard about Ingo from Russell Targ and was glad to meet him. We liked each other immediately, so when Alan and George dropped out, Ingo was the first person who came to mind, and he suggested Hella. From that point on, Ingo was a Mobius Society [Schwartz's research group] remote viewer.

"He used to stay with me and my family when he came down to Los Angeles to the Scientology center. We spent a lot of time together. He was an interesting man. Very smart, author of several interesting books, a good writer, and a really good remote viewer. He was gay and had been bullied as a boy. As a man, it gave him an edge, and he had no trouble asserting himself. When he was retained by the Army to teach remote viewing, he and Hal created the Coordinate Remote Viewing (CRV) protocol still associated with the Star Gate SRI program. Ingo was the authority over these Army men who, as boys, might have bullied him. He saw the irony in that, and took satisfaction from it. Ingo, perhaps as much as any of us scientists, shaped the form of remote viewing. He was, in fact, the one who coined the term, and he gave us the understanding of how it works. Ingo Swann was the father of remote viewing."

CHAPTER 2

Helena Blavatsky: Clairvoyance in the 19th Century

Helena Blavatsky   Charles Leadbeater   Annie Besant

Figure 7. Founders of the Theosophical Society in 1875

B orn in 1831, Helena Blavatsky was a Russian author, spiritualist, and philosopher. She became the leading theoretician of Theosophy and co-founded the Theosophical Society in New York City in 1875. Her goal was to "investigate the laws of nature and the powers latent in man." The "powers latent in man" that she wrote about and researched included physic powers, telepathy, and clairvoyance. These abilities are the antecedents of remote viewing through space and time that we used in our program, and what remote viewers still use today.

Having lived in India, where she studied Buddhist and Hindu philosophies, Blavatsky believed that Theosophy, as brought to her by enlightened Himalayan masters (with whom she remained in contact after she returned to Europe from her adventures in India), was the intersection of science, religion, and philosophy. She believed in the essential oneness of all beings and felt that ancient wisdom from an unknowable divine source preceded and underlay all religions. Even today, nearly one hundred and fifty years later, there are Theosophical Society branches in major cities all over the world. The one I belonged to was the beautiful New York City branch on East 53rd Street. I will have more to say about that in chapter 9.

In 1895, Blavatsky asked her powerful psychic colleagues, Charles Leadbeater and Annie Besant, to help create a psychic periodic table of the elements. They were asked to clairvoyantly visualize atomic particles and show their structure, starting with the element hydrogen. The target object was a block of paraffin, which is 98 percent hydrogen.

On the left of Figure 8 is a copy of the original 1895 drawing from the theosophical magazine, *Lucifer*, showing a hydrogen molecule as perceived psychically and drawn by Charles Leadbeater. Looking at the block of paraffin, he identified three "tiny spheres of fundamental matter, held together by three bands of energy." On the right is a contemporary drawing of a proton, showing two up-quarks and one down-quark, held together by gluons. Protons were discovered by Ernest Rutherford, but not until 1918. Quarks were predicted by Murray Gell-Mann, but not until 1964. It appears that consciousness

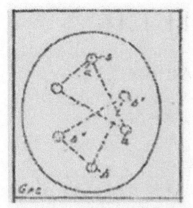 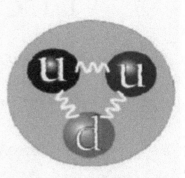

Figure 8. An 1895 psychic drawing of a hydrogen atom,
and a modern drawing with quarks

permeates everything, independent of distance, *whether it is 500 million miles to Jupiter or 10^{-10} cm to a hydrogen molecule.* This could be considered the first documented instance of remote viewing.

The modern periodic table of the elements was created by Russian chemist Dmitri Mendeleev in 1869. Annie Besant wrote the 1895 article #5, titled "Occult Chemistry," with the purpose of beginning work on a psychic periodic table. Besant and Leadbeater wrote a large book of the same name in 1908. In it, they psychically described many other elements.

Besant met fellow theosophist Charles Leadbeater in London in April 1894. They became close co-workers in the theosophical movement and would remain close friends for the rest of their lives. Leadbeater claimed clairvoyance from childhood (like Ingo Swann), and as an artist he wrote and colorfully illustrated many beautiful books illuminating his psychic views of living and non-living specimens. He helped Besant become clairvoyant herself in the following year. In a

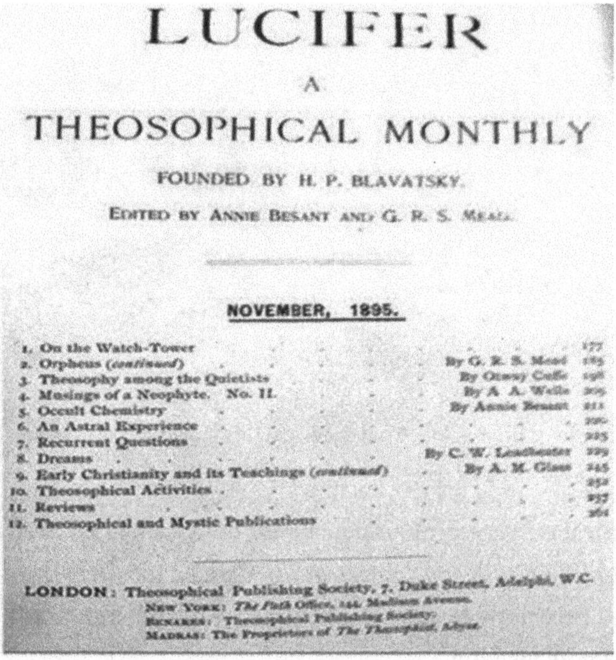

LUCIFER

A

THEOSOPHICAL MONTHLY

FOUNDED BY H. P. BLAVATSKY.

EDITED BY ANNIE BESANT AND G. R. S. MEAD.

NOVEMBER, 1895.

LONDON: Theosophical Publishing Society, 7, Duke Street, Adelphi, W.C.
NEW YORK: *The Path Office*, 144, Madison Avenue.
BENARES: Theosophical Publishing Society.
MADRAS: The Proprietors of *The Theosophist*, Adyar.

Figure 9. Table of contents from *Lucifer* magazine

letter dated 25 August 1895 to Francisca Arundale, Leadbeater narrates how Besant became profoundly clairvoyant. The letter describes how together they clairvoyantly investigated "the universe, matter, thought-forms, and the history of mankind" and co-authored *Occult Chemistry.*

The cover of their now famous 1908 book describes "Investigations by Clairvoyant Magnification into the Structure of the Atoms of the Periodic Table and of Some Compounds." It presents "clairvoyant observations of the chemical Elements." At the time the book was written, Besant and Leadbeater were leaders of the Theosophical Society branch based in Adyar,

India. Besant was the president of the Society, having succeeded the Society's co-founder, Henry Olcott, after his death in 1907.

I joined the Theosophical Society in 1956, shortly before leaving Columbia. Seeing the remarkable 1895 *Lucifer* article, as a physicist, I, along with other scientists who were members of the Society at that time, had the idea that these people had really been on to something—remember, that was sixty-nine years before quarks were predicted by Gell-Mann.

Besant and Leadbeater were some of the first people in the world to apply clairvoyance for purposes of gaining scientific information. In 1995, electrical engineering professor Stephen M. Phillips wrote a scientific review of their book *Occult Chemistry* in the *Journal of Scientific Exploration*. His review is called, "Extrasensory Perception of Subatomic Particles." I am including his abstract here. He also wrote a book, *Extrasensory Perception of Quarks*, in the same year as the *Journal of Scientific Exploration* article.

ABSTRACT: A century-old claim by two early leaders of the Theosophical Society to have used a form of ESP to observe subatomic particles is evaluated. Their 1895 observations are found to be consistent with facts of nuclear physics and with the quark model of particle physics provided that their assumption that they "saw" atoms is rejected. Their account of the force binding together the fundamental constituents of matter is shown to agree with the string model. Their description of these basic particles bears striking similarity to basic ideas of superstring theory. The implication of this remarkable correlation between ostensible paranormal observations of subatomic particles and facts of nuclear and particle physics is that quarks are neither fundamental nor hadronic states of superstrings, as many physicists currently assume, but instead, are composed of three subquark states of a superstring.[1]

CHAPTER 3

Pat Price: The Psychic Policeman

Figure 10. Pat Price, retired police commissioner and outstanding psychic

Pat Price was a remarkably psychic retired police commissioner from Burbank, California. We were grateful for his participation in our program. He came to us with a large scrapbook of newspaper clippings attesting to his psychic prowess in his capacity as police commissioner. It's a little mysterious how he heard about our secret program, but within a few weeks he had secured clearance.

In Pat's first remote viewing trial at Stanford Research Institute, he psychically "looked for" our colleague, Hal

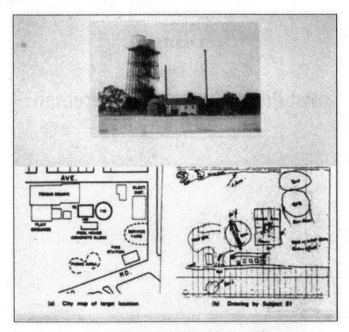

Figure 11. Pat Price's drawing of the Rinconada
swimming pool complex in Palo Alto, California

Puthoff, and our CIA contract monitor, Dr. Kit Green, who
had left the premises. As Pat and I sat together in an electri-
cally shielded cage, called a screen room, I asked Pat to tell
me about his impressions regarding Hal's location. Pat said
to me, "I don't know what you're talking about." Since I knew
that Pat had a whole scrapbook full of newspaper clippings of
his having caught crooks on the streets of Burbank, I instead
asked him to track the pair as he would have in his police
work. I prompted him to remember that Hal and Kit had left
the SRI parking lot in Hal's green Honda Accord. Then I asked
Pat if he could "just follow the green car," which we of course
couldn't physically see from our sequestered location. Pat said,

"Yes, I see them leaving the parking lot, and turning south onto Middlefield Road. They are driving into a park."

This illustrates the part that an interviewer can play in a remote viewing session. If I weren't with Pat to jolly him along, it would have been a failed session, rather than the great success it was. Pat's drawing on the bottom right (facing page) closely approximates the city map shown on the bottom left. He clearly illustrates a rectangular pool 60 x 80 feet and a round pool to the left of it, 100 feet in diameter. The target location was the Rinconada swimming pool complex in Palo Alto, California. Both drawing dimensions are accurate to within 10 percent. The large side-by-side water tanks in the upper right corner of his drawing weren't there at the time, but they used to be there. I didn't learn about the water tanks until ten years after the experiment.

In the first experiments we did with Pat, we conducted nine more double-blind remote viewings. After each of Pat's verbal descriptions of a distant target, he would make a written transcript of his impressions along with any pictures he felt inclined to draw. These nine transcripts would be randomly numbered from one to nine. A judge would then be given the set of transcripts and a set of the nine traveling orders that had been issued to the "outbound experimenter," who could have been directed to any one of sixty different locations in the Bay Area.

The outbound experimenter would go to a different location each time. Randomly, you would expect a judge to correctly match the description in one of the nine transcripts with one of the nine outbound traveling orders. That is, you would expect to get one out of nine just by chance. In this

Target Location	Distance (km)	Rank of Associated Transcript
Hoover Tower, Stanford	3.4	1
Baylands Nature Preserve	6.4	1
Radio telescope, Portola Valley	6.4	1
Marina, Redwood City	6.8	1
Bridge toll plaza, Fremont	14.5	6
Drive-in theater, Palo Alto	5.1	1
Arts and Crafts Plaza, Menlo Park	1.9	1
Catholic Church, Portola Valley	8.5	3
Swimming pool complex, Palo Alto	3.4	1
TOTAL SUM OF RANKS		16 (p = 2.9 x 10⁻⁵)

Table 1. Rankings 1–9, assigned by judges to each of
Pat Price's nine transcripts (probability value of 2.9 x 10⁻⁵)

case, they matched seven of the nine. The chance of that is one in 100,000. Therefore, Pat's series of nine trials was statistically significant at one in 100,000. That is to say, if Hal, for example, had been kidnapped nine times in a row, Pat would have found him the first place he looked seven out of the nine times.

Price also had his whimsical side. I remember once when one of our cheerful secretaries who had been typing up Pat's transcripts asked him if he could close his eyes and follow her into the ladies' room. Pat answered her, "If I can focus my

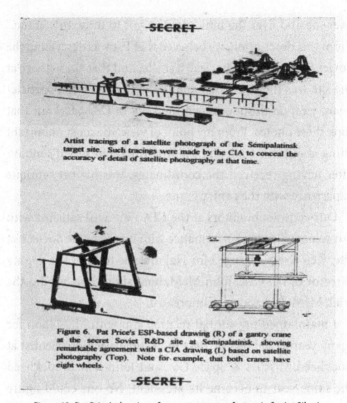

Figure 12. Pat Price's drawing of a secret weapons factory in Soviet Siberia

attention to any place on the planet, why would I want to follow you into the ladies' room?" Why Indeed?

In another remote viewing series of trials, Pat correctly described a giant gantry crane as "having eight wheels, and rolling over a building where important construction was going on." In this experiment, Pat was given only the geographic coordinates, latitude and longitude. As Pat started his description of this site, he said, "I am lying on my back on top of a three-story building at the site. The sun feels good on my body. As I look up, I see a giant gantry crane rolling

over me and over the building. I've got to draw this crane."
From this description, we believed that Pat was describing the
Soviet Semipalatinsk nuclear test site, and that the activity at
the site was the construction and development of a particle-
beam weapon to shoot down the kind of US spacecraft that
took these photos. From my point of view, the most important
thing about this trial, and the first thing out of Pat's mouth
after having received the coordinates, was his very unique
experience with the gantry crane.

Our contract monitors at the CIA were well satisfied with
our remote viewing performance with regard to the Soviet test
site. Ken Kress arranged for Hal and me to brief the deputy
director of the CIA, John McMahon, about how we did the
trial. McMahon was very impressed.

I maintained my cordial relationship with McMahon for
many years. I left SRI in 1982 to become a senior scientist at
Lockheed Missiles & Space Co., and John joined Lockheed
the same year to become its president. No one could figure
out why, in this 25,000 person company, John was always so
accommodating to me. But they were unaware of our past
secret relationship at the CIA.

After Price drew the gantry crane, the CIA asked for more
details. They wanted him to look into the building under the
crane to see what they were constructing. We went back into
our shielded room and Pat immediately started describing a
huge steel sphere under construction, made from gores shaped
like orange peel slices.

This was unknown to the CIA at the time. Pat said that
the steel was so thick that they were having trouble welding it together. Additionally, he noted that there were many

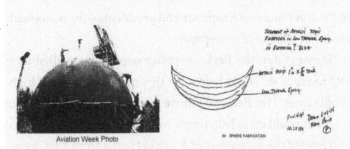

Figure 13. Price correctly described gores used to create sixty-foot steel spheres

people in white coats, speaking languages other than Russian. Interestingly, he was not only able to see the gores, but he also was intuitively aware of the processes taking place. All the construction, including the welding problems, was later revealed and confirmed in a 1977 *Aviation Week* article. It was unknown at the time Price drew it. In fact, much of what Pat Price described in this viewing was unknown to the intelligence community until after his death in 1975.

On the night of Monday, February 4, 1974, a group of American terrorists kidnapped nineteen-year-old newspaper heiress Patricia Hearst from her apartment near the University of California in Berkeley, where she was a student. The kidnappers identified themselves as the Symbionese Liberation Army (SLA). They were radical anarchists whose oft-repeated slogan was "Death to the fascist insect that preys upon the life of the people." The conservative and wealthy Hearst family was a perfect target for them. While the press was trying to find "Symbia" on the map, the Berkeley police department was trying to locate the daughter of one of the most prominent celebrities in the city of San Francisco—namely the publisher of the *San Francisco Examiner* and president of the nationwide Hearst syndicate of newspapers.

The next day, the Berkeley police department called us at SRI to see if we could help with this most troubling of high-profile cases. Hal, Pat, and I drove north to Berkeley to find out what Pat could do to help them. As it turned out, Pat identified and *named* the kidnapper of Patricia Hearst from a fat, loose-leaf "mug book" filled with hundreds of photos. He stood at a large oak table in the station house and turned the pages of the mug book, one by one. He then put his finger on the face of a man and announced, "That's the ringleader." The man he fingered was Donald DeFreeze, who was indeed identified as the ringleader within the week. Pat also said, "There is a Mr. Lobo." One week later, accomplice Willie Wolfe was identified by the police. He was known to the gang as Lobo.

The detective in charge then asked Pat if he had any idea where they were now—the most famous query of all movie lawmen, "Which way'd they go?" Pat said, "They went that way," pointing north. He said, "I see a white station wagon near a restaurant. It's across the highway from two large white gas storage tanks, near an overpass." One of the detectives said, "I know where that is. It's on the way to Vallejo where I live." The detectives then dispatched a police cruiser.

Within ten minutes it radioed back that they had found the kidnap car fifteen miles to the north of us. The car still had spent cartridges rolling around on the floor—the same caliber of shells seen earlier in the day on the bedroom floor of Hearst's Berkeley apartment. There was no doubt they had found the right car. This experience in the police station where, right in front of me, Price identified the kidnapper and then located the kidnap car is one of the strongest reasons that I believe in ESP. How could I not?! How about you?

The police found the car, but they didn't find the kidnappers or Patty Hearst. The next day we assembled again at the station house. The police wanted to canvass the Berkeley hills behind the university. One of the officers chose me to accompany him to examine an abandoned farm house high in the hills. As we pulled up to a ramshackle building, the policeman pulled out his service revolver and asked if I could cover his back when he kicked in the door. He asked, "Do you know how to use one of these?" I replied that, in fact, I owned a Walther automatic. So, the policeman handed me his heavy .38 loaded with lead. I had to laugh to myself that this policeman had no idea he had just handed his gun to Mr. Magoo with the idea that I would cover his back. Lucky for us all, it didn't come to that. We received a letter of thanks and commendation from the Berkeley Police Department for our efforts during the several days we worked with them.

In 1974, Pat Price worked with me to describe where Hal Puthoff was located each day at noon. Hal had gone on vacation to South America and we tracked him daily. On four successive days, Price described Hal's whereabouts as being at a harbor, a market, a volcano, and a church. On day five, Price did not show up for the remote viewing trial. I didn't know it then, but I was going to have to get used to not working with Pat Price.

At the appointed time, I said into the tape recorder, "This is a remote viewing with Pat Price and Russ Targ." After a few

Figure 14. Russell Targ and Hal Puthoff, co-founders of SRI remote viewing program

minutes I said, "Pat doesn't appear to be coming, so I will have to try it myself. . . . I see grass and sand on the right, and some kind of airport building on the left. And there appears to be ocean at the end of a runway. I think I will make a drawing. It looks to me like an island airport." That drawing and a later photograph is shown to the right. I include this trial to illustrate that remote viewing is so easy and natural that even a scientist can do it.

Later that year, Hal and I published our first paper in *Nature*, celebrating Pat's great success with remote viewing.[1]

So what had happened to Pat? After helping with the Patty Hearst case and describing the Soviet weapons factory in Siberia, Price was recruited directly by the CIA and went to West

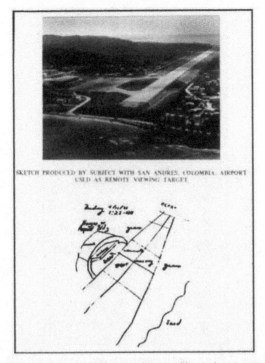

Figure 15. Russell Targ's psychic drawing of San Andres airport

Figure 16. Modern photo of San Andres airport

Coal Executive Proud To Be West Virginian

By HARRY L. BAISDEN
Herald Dispatch Staff Writer

Figure 17. Price is urged to move east to work directly with the CIA

Virginia to work directly with them on operational trials. Unfortunately, he died mysteriously in 1975 at age fifty-six. Pat had strongly believed his life was in danger prior to this and had given his wife a million-dollar term-life insurance policy before he had come to visit us at SRI. We don't know if he had a heart attack or was killed, either by the Russians (who knew full well what he was up to) or by the CIA (who had discovered that Pat was passing secret material to his Scientology church). This latter fact was revealed by CIA agents Ken Kress and Kit Green in my film *Third Eye Spies*. It was also reported in the *New York Times*. I have to ask, "What do you do if you discover that Superman is a double agent?"

CHAPTER 4

Hella Hammid:
A Very Psychic Control

Figure 18. Hella Hammid was a very successful and surprising remote viewer

Hella Hammid was a distinguished professional photographer. She was an open-hearted, beautiful, artistic, and highly intelligent friend of my family for many years. She was chosen as a "control" viewer at CIA request, because she had no previous ESP experience. In a series of nine trials to describe the location of a hidden person, she was statistically significant at odds of almost 1 in 1,000,000.

My good friend and colleague Stephan Schwartz, the archeologist and remote viewing researcher who worked with Ingo Swann, also worked with Hella. He worked with her all over the world for two decades, from the depths of an underwater investigation near Santa Catalina Island to the heat of the Egyptian desert. His memories of our dear friend are as follows:

"As a girl she was a refugee, part of an affluent Jewish family that fled the Nazis on a day's notice as Hitler took control of Germany. She was educated at one of England's finest boarding schools for girls, and the mix of refugee and English boarding school made her gracious, self-assured, and adventurous. Russell Targ told me he had brought her into the SRI program originally as a control, until it became clear she was an exceptional remote viewer. If you had been introduced to her at a party, they would have told you she was a nationally known fine arts photographer. And after spending a few minutes with her you would have seen she was distinctly feminist, a woman aware of nonlocal consciousness, but in no way woowoo. In 1977, I asked her to participate in the remote viewing submarine experiments known as Deep Quest, and she not only located a previously unknown wreck on the seafloor, but drew a picture and described an utterly unpredictable large stone block that would be found at the site. And it was found there.

"That was Hella's specialty. She loved to describe something no one expected or even imagined. The stone block in Deep

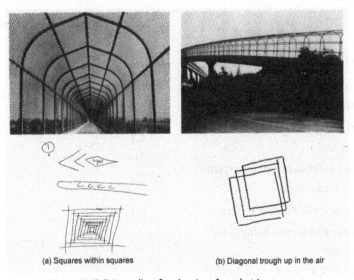

(a) Squares within squares   (b) Diagonal trough up in the air

Figure 19. Hella's excellent first drawing of a pedestrian overpass

Quest; a column and cistern in Alexandria, Egypt; details of the remains of Columbus's fourth voyage caravel in Jamaica. As she had been at SRI, and at my lab, Mobius, Hella became part of the solid base of remote viewers that made the practical application of remote viewing in archaeology possible. We worked together and traveled all over the world on expeditions until her death from breast cancer. Very little fazed her. She was always fun to be with, and it was a striking experience to watch her remote view a site, and then see how startlingly accurate she was."

In Hella's first remote viewing trial, I asked her to quiet her mind and describe the surprising images that appeared in her awareness. She described something "moving fast." I suggested we take a break. She then described "a trough up in the air. But it couldn't hold water, because it was full of holes." I

Target Location	Distance (km)	Rank of Associated Transcript
Methodist Church, Palo Alto	1.9	1
Ness Auditorium, Menlo Park	0.2	1
Merry-go-round, Palo Alto	3.4	1
Parking garage, Mountain View	8.1	2
SRI International Courtyard, Menlo Park	0.2	1
Bicycle shed, Menlo Park	0.1	2
Railroad trestle bridge, Palo Alto	1.3	2
Pumpkin patch, Menlo Park	1.3	1
Pedestrian overpass, Palo Alto	5.0	2
TOTAL SUM OF RANKS		13 (p = 1.8 x 10-6)

Table 2. Rankings 1–9, assigned by judges to each of Hella Hammid's nine transcripts (probability value of 1.8 x 10-6)

then suggested she draw what she was seeing. She said, "There are squares, within squares, within squares," and she made the final drawing. The target location was a pedestrian overpass over Highway 101 in Palo Alto.

We did eight more trials like this with Hella. Although she didn't draw with the exactitude of Pat Price, her drawings almost never contained things that were incorrect. In her series of nine trials, she had five first-place matches and four second-places matches, but everything was so well done that overall her statistical significance was almost one in a million. As a result, we published our second paper in the *Proceeding of the IEEE*, celebrating Hella's great success.[1]

For us, the conclusion of this series of trials showed that sometimes an inexperienced viewer can produce results that are more significant than a lifetime psychic. What we see is that while the very remarkable Pat Price did an experiment that was significant at one in 100,000, our delightful control subject, Hella Hammid, did a similar experiment that was significant at nearly one in a million.

After almost a decade of work, Hella's descriptions became increasingly accurate—the opposite of a "decline effect," as was often seen in J. B. Rhine's experiments using the five different type of Zener cards (star, circle, etc.). One day we did an experiment for which I told her that we didn't have a person at the target, but we had the geographical coordinates of the site instead. I showed her the coordinates of latitude and longitude, which were in binary form—1s and 0s instead of the usual degrees, minutes, and seconds. As always, I had no idea of the target. All remote viewing trials at SRI were double blind.

What Hella got to see was a file card showing something like the following: 10010100110-N and 11001001101-W. The coordinates were prepared by physicist Ed May, who had joined our program in 1976. Hella commented, "That's an interesting looking pattern." Then she closed her eyes, gave a great sigh (which was always a sign of good psi for her), and said, "I see some kind of round structure." She laughed and continued, "It looks like a belly-button shaped energy expander. There are three rays coming out of it."

Then she requested some clay to make a model of what she saw. She felt that the new medium would allow her an additional mode of expression for what she was experiencing. The

         Third Eye Spies

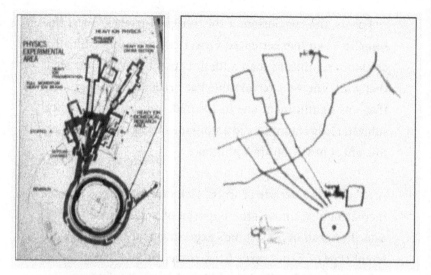

Figure 20: Berkeley Bevatron target. On the left is the official schematic showing the circular accelerator and beam tubes. Hella's drawing is on the right. She described "A belly-button shaped, energy expander, with highly illuminated rays shooting out."

target was the UC Berkeley Bevatron—a hollow, circular particle accelerator which is, indeed, an "energy expander" that has four beam tubes leading to the experimental labs, or target buildings. The illustration in Figure 20 shows the remarkable similarity between her drawing and the beam tubes, and the accelerator fifty miles away. Figure 21 shows her clay model of the surprising images appearing in her awareness.

With Hella, we often saw this kind of almost magical connection between the function and form of the target. At the end of a decade of this kind of remote viewing, I began to think of her as our oracle, who would often say words to which she attached no particular meaning. One day when the target was the Stanford Linear Accelerator, she saw "polished metal tubes or cylinders. . . . This has something to do with a

Figure 21. Hella's clay model of Berkeley Bevatron, showing belly-button energy expander, beam tubes, and target building

trajectory," she said. Such a description is entirely appropriate for an electron accelerator.

We now know that an important ingredient of our remote viewing success is derived from the rapport between the remote viewer and interviewer—acting together as a single information-gathering team. The remote viewer's role is that of perceiver and information channel. The interviewer's role is designed to be that of an analytical control. From my point of view, the interviewer is a kind of psychic travel agent. My first job as the interviewer is to help the remote viewer to silence the ongoing mental chatter—the mental noise. "Monkey mind," as the Buddhists say.

This division of labor between viewer and interviewer mirrors the two primary modes of cerebral functioning as we understand them. One is the *nonanalytical* thinking style that is predominant in spatial pattern recognition and other holistic processing, which is thought to be a major component of psi functioning. The other is the *analytical* cognitive style that characterizes verbal and other goal-oriented reasoning processes. Only very experienced remote viewers appear to have the ability to handle both cognitive styles simultaneously. This nonanalytical, or artistic, functioning is sometimes considered to be indicative of "right-brain" activity.

In 1982, Hella and I were asked by Ken Kress, our CIA contract monitor, to "take a look at Premier Brezhnev's office in the Kremlin." Hella lay down on a couch, and I sat nearby with my tape recorder. Hella described walking down a wide hall draped in red. She said, "I am coming to some double doors covered with red leather, held in place by large upholstery tacks. But the door is closed." I said to her, "I will open the door," as though I was guiding someone in a lucid dream. Hella said, "It's night time and the room is dark." I said, "I'll turn on the lights." Hella said, "I see a large wooden desk covered with glass. It's on the right. On the left is a window that seems to be looking out on Red Square. I see Saint Basil's cathedral. And behind the desk, I see a wooden door in the wall." I said, "I'll open it, and we can see where it leads."

We agreed to go through the doorway and down some stairs. Hella said that there was a "large computer room on the right." At that point I became frightened. I told Hella that I have lots of clearances, but I am not cleared to be in a computer room in the Kremlin. I proposed to end the session, which we did. It was like the end of a somewhat disconcerting shared out-of-body experience.

Figure 22. Representations of Hella's description of
Brezhnev's red doors and view from his window

The following year, I left SRI. I was invited to give a talk on my non-classified remote viewing experiments to the Academy of Sciences of the Soviet Union. My talk was very well received. I explained to the audience that "with remote viewing it is not possible to hide anything anymore. No more secrets!" People were shocked, and there was a great rattling of tea cups. I was asked if there was anything I would like to see in the Kremlin, which is where we were. I said that I would like to see Premier Brezhnev's office, where he sits. They walked me down a hall hung with red banners. We then came to a door covered with red leather, just as Hella had described. When we walked into Brezhnev's office, I could see his large wooden desk on the right and a vista of Red Square out the window on the left. I do not recall if there was a door behind his desk as Hella had mentioned. Everything else was just as Hella had described.

CHAPTER 5

Gary Langford: An Engineer for All Seasons

Figure 23. Gary Langford teaching at the Naval Post Graduate School

After four years in the laboratory, I finally had an opportunity to switch from interviewer to outbound experimenter to visit a distant site personally. I chose to travel to New Orleans to visit a friend who was in medical school there. The people at SRI had no idea what city I was traveling to. To start our trial, I purchased a New Orleans picture book from a street vender and threw a die on the pavement to randomly select a target location to visit. I was sent to the Louisiana Superdome.

I stood in front of the building and described my location into my tape recorder. I said that the time was noon, and the building was shining like a UFO in the noonday sun. That would turn out to be a bad choice of words! Meanwhile at SRI, my friend and colleague Elizabeth Rauscher was the interviewer conducting the experiment. Elizabeth was a theoretical physics professor at the University of California, Berkeley. The viewer was an SRI engineer named Gary Langford, who had never done an experiment with us before, though he said he'd had many psychic experiences in his life. He told us that as a high school student, he had played baseball in the outfield because his ESP would often tell him where the ball would arrive. That was his qualification to be in our program. He told Elizabeth that my site looked like a UFO. "Do you think Russell has been abducted?" Gary asked. Elizabeth said, "You can never tell. Just draw what you see." Gary then made the two excellent drawings shown on the next page.

My next stop after the Superdome was to visit my father in New York City. Together with him and my daughter, Elisabeth, we visited Grant's Tomb, a famous monument on Riverside Drive. Gary told his interviewer that I seemed to be going into a building with pillars on the front. He said that I seemed to be asking someone to help me make change. In fact, it was my daughter who went into the building to purchase the photograph that I show in Figure 25 (along with Gary's drawing).

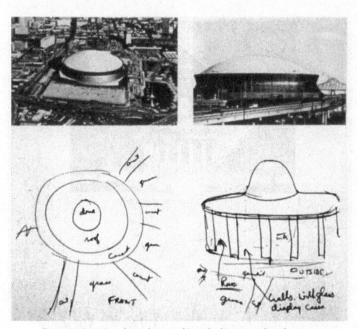

Figure 24. Louisiana Superdome and Langford's outstanding drawings

The following year, in 1979, Gary played a key role in locating a Russian Tu-22 bomber that had crashed in Africa. It was hidden by the jungle so that it could not be seen by satellite photography. Working with Dale Graff from the Defense Intelligence Agency (DIA) and another remote viewer, Rosemary Smith (an airman from Wright-Patterson Air Force Base), Gary was able to mark a map with a three-mile-radius circle, showing mountains, a river, and a village. He then provided a more detailed description of the specific location, indicating hills in the distance, a muddy river, and heavy jungle foliage that concealed the plane. He even showed the plane sticking out of the river.

GRANT'S TOMB TARGET IN NEW YORK CITY

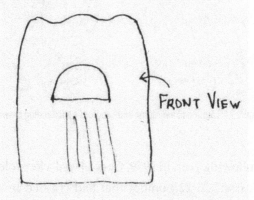

FRONT VIEW

Figure 25. Grant's Tomb and Langford's drawing from 3,000 miles distance

When the CIA arrived in their unauthorized helicopter at Gary's location in Zaire, they were immediately able to find the specific location. They saw villagers dragging parts of the plane out of the jungle, just where Gary had marked the map to indicate the crash site. They even recovered the precious reconnaissance code books. President Jimmy Carter confirms this whole event in the opening scene of my 2018 documentary film, *Third Eye Spies*.

CHAPTER 6

Joe McMoneagle: Government Remote Viewer 001 (and Other Government Viewers)

Figure 26. Joe McMoneagle, a decade of successful remote viewing with the Army

The Army wanted to create its own psychic corps so that it wouldn't have to come to California when it needed help in finding a kidnapped officer or a downed Russian plane. Joe McMoneagle was a warrant officer with the US Army Intelligence and Security Command (INSCOM) when I selected him from a group of thirty candidates offered to us by the

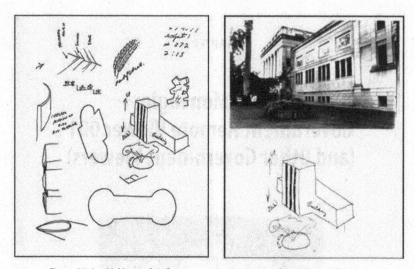

Figure 27. Joe McMoneagle's first remote viewing among the six Army volunteers

Army to join the remote viewing program in 1978. Joe had had many psychic experiences in Vietnam during his combat duty, so I had no problem selecting him as one of our six trainees.

In my work with Joe at SRI, he achieved five first-place matches out of six trials in our initial training. He was not only an excellent remote viewer but also an accomplished artist, which made him exceptionally valuable to the Army program. This decade of work is described in his fascinating book, *Memoirs of a Psychic Spy: The Remarkable Life of US Government Remote Viewer 001*.

In Joe's first remote viewing experience with us, my research partner Hal Puthoff was sent to an undisclosed location in the area. As I sat with Joe in the shielded room, I asked him to describe the location where Hal had gone. Joe covered a page with a number of small sketches, shown on the left in Figure

27. I told him that a judge would have a hard time selecting from among his many drawings. Could he take another look in his mental awareness and see if his images came together? He then made the drawing on the right and described the target as a "tall building and a short building, with the tall building designed to look like piano keys." Indeed, the judge had no difficulty in correctly matching Joe's excellent drawing to the Stanford Art Museum.

A dozen years after Joe drew the Stanford Art Museum, he was called upon to offer a demonstration of his ability. This would help support a pitch for the continuation of the remote viewing program that the Army and CIA were still interested in after Hal and I left SRI in the early 1980s. The new follow-on program was conducted by Dr. Ed May at the Science Applications International Corporation (SAIC), a private "think tank" like SRI.

For the test, the CIA sent an outbound experimenter to SAIC. He conducted the experiment as two trials to see if energy sources would make especially good remote viewing targets, such as a windmill farm or an atomic bomb factory. The CIA experimenter would leave Ed's laboratory and arrive somewhere at 10:00 a.m., remain there for a while, go to a second site at noon, and then return to the lab. These were, of course, still double blind trials.

The first site was the Altamonte windmill farm about fifty miles east of SAIC. Joe, a very good remote viewing artist, described tall towers, an electrical grid, and something rotating. The second site was the Lawrence Livermore National Laboratory, our own atomic bomb factory, about a hundred miles east of Ed's lab. Joe correctly described a six-story,

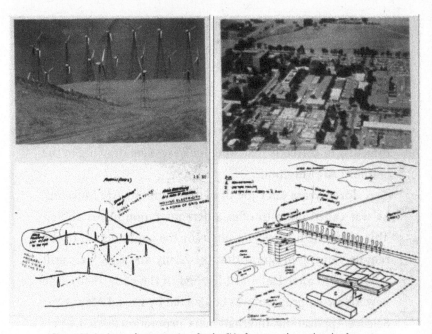

Figure 28. Joe's two demonstrations for the CIA after more than a decade of remote viewing; (left) Altamonte windmill farm, (right) Lawrence Livermore nuclear site

T-shaped building covered with glass, and a long row of trees next to the building. Joe showed no loss of ability after more than ten years of more or less continual practice of remote viewing. Remote viewing is an ability that does not get worn out with use. There is no decline effect.

In 1978, we did six remote viewing trials with each of our six Army volunteers. We would expect each of them, at random, to achieve one first-place match out of six trials. Thus we could expect a total of six first-place matches out of our thirty-six trials. Because remote viewing is widely available, and our viewers were highly motivated Army officers, they obtained

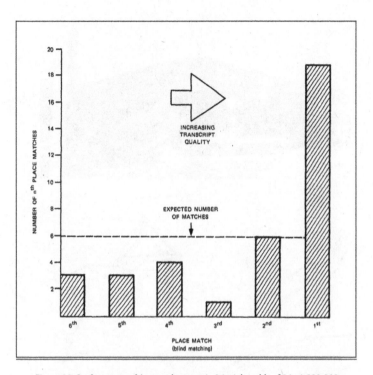

Figure 29. Performance of Army volunteers in 36 trials, odds of 1 in 1,000,000

nineteen first-place matches, which is significant at almost one in a million. These six officers went on to make up the core of the Army program that continued to do active remote viewing for a decade, comprising hundreds of operational tasks for the CIA and DIA and many other governmental intelligence organizations.

After our thirty-six trials with the Army volunteers, we noticed that one of the men, Hartleigh Trent, kept describing the site of the next day, which was of course counted as a miss. He had worked with J. B. Rhine, the founder of parapsychology in America, out of Duke University, and was quite familiar

Figure 30. Test of precognition with an Army volunteer

with precognition. Hartleigh made an interesting proposal to me and Dr. Charles Tart, a distinguished psychology professor from UC Davis who was consulting with our program. Hartleigh asked that we let him describe a future target that we would randomly choose *after* he made his description. Hartleigh recorded his description and called down to a distant trailer where Charley Tart and I were waiting.

Charley handed me a Kodak carousel projector with sixty slides and said, "Okay, Russ, it's up to you." I rotated the carousel and pushed the projector button. The slide that appeared was a Ford dealership on El Camino Real, not far from SRI. Hartleigh then came to see us and played his tape, where he described a building with a "glass front, and a very tall pointed roof like a castle." He said, "Somewhere at the site is a large star." In fact, we saw a large star in the window of the dealership when we visited, which was positive feedback for his excellent precognitive viewing.

Toward the end of our program, we were visited by a cheerful young woman from the CIA, who was tasked to see if there were any sensory leaks in our protocol that could provide a normal explanation for our remote viewing data of the past several years. Her name was Francine, and she had a PhD in mechanical engineering, earned prior to her enlistment in the CIA. She told me that she had joined the CIA specifically to investigate the crazy-seeming program that they were supporting with us.

I did two remote viewing hide-and-go-seek trials with her, where she served as the remote viewer. Hal was again sent out to find a location somewhere in the San Francisco Bay area, and Francine attempted to describe that place. She was surprisingly successful in these trials. But she said that she couldn't really trust me. I might be giving her clues, or whispering the correct answer!

Francine's plan was to do a remote viewing session by herself, without an interviewer, with earplugs in her ears. Hal and I would go together to our randomly chosen site and take pictures and make a recording to see if her sequestered drawing would match our target. Since we didn't trust her either, we taped the laboratory door closed from the outside, using

duct tape. We then went to the departmental office and asked
the secretary to generate a random number with her HP cal-
culator. Using that number, she would then go through the
stack of sixty driving instructions and give us the directions
that corresponded to the number. All of this is our usual
practice. The location she came up with was the "merry-go-
round in Rinconada Park," the same site as the swimming
pools that had been chosen to start our program many years
earlier.

When Hal and I got there, we made a recording of all the
children shouting, "Push me, push me." And we took many
photos of the merry-go-round in the children's park. When we
returned, we found our tape job on the door was still intact,
and Francine was waiting for us with a handful of drawings.
When we asked what she had drawn, she couldn't tell us. She
said it was like a "cupula." And she couldn't tell us what that
meant.

Years later, my daughter Elisabeth, who was a psychiatrist
and Russian translator, was interviewing a famous Russian
psychic, Djuna Davidashvili, in Moscow, with regard to where
our American colleague was hiding in San Francisco. The only
word I recognized in the half-hour interview was the Russian
word "cupula." The target was also a merry-go-round!

In our SRI experiment Francine said, "There is some sort of
steel structure going round a central post." We show our photograph of the site on the left, together with Francine's drawing on the right. Over our long friendship with Francine, we
learned that she was not at all the naive subject she pretended
to be when she walked into our lab. In fact, she had had psychic experiences all her life. The agency was very impressed

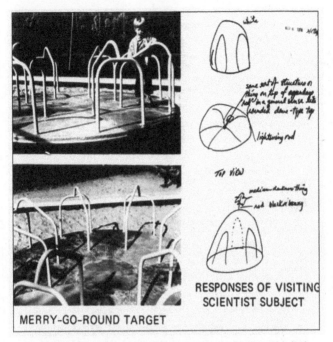

Figure 31. The CIA takes a look at the merry-go-round in Rinconada Park

Figure 32. Original logo of Grill Flame

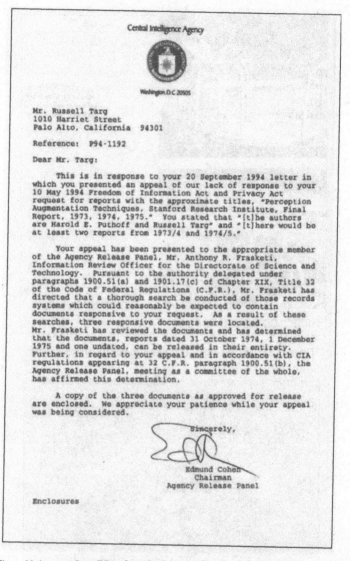

Figure 33. Letter to Russell Targ from the CIA giving him permission to reveal previously classified material from the SRI remote viewing program

with her success, and she became co-manager of a stand alone remote viewing program at CIA after the program at SRI was shut down.

The original 1973 classified code-word name for our program at SRI was Grill Flame. The Grill Flame logo is shown on page 53, drawn by an unknown Army artist.

The eventual name for the program, as taken over by the Army at Fort Meade in 1978, was Star Gate. Project Star Gate was declassified in 1995 due to the work of my son, attorney Nicholas Targ, which is how I can write about it today.

CHAPTER 7

Precognition: No Time Like the Future

For us believing physicists, the distinction between
past, present and future is only an illusion, even if a
stubborn one.

—ALBERT EINSTEIN, 3/21/1955,
TO THE CHILDREN OF HIS GOOD FRIEND
MICHELE BESSO, AFTER BESSO'S DEATH

Einstein wrote numerous articles and essays about our misunderstanding of the nature of time. Physicists have no meter with which to measure the passage of time, like the flow of a river as it passes and turns a paddlewheel. A clock simply counts the clicks and ticks of an escapement; it doesn't have anything to say about the passage of time. However, as we float down our imaginary river of time, we can sometimes see turbulence up ahead—perhaps it is caused by boulders out of sight just beyond a bend in the river. Thus, the white water gives us a premonitory glimpse of future trouble up ahead.

The evidence is very strong that we can learn to become aware of these glimpses brought to us by our *nonlocal awareness* beyond space and time. Precognition or premonitions refer to this awareness, either conscious or unconscious, of future events that cannot be inferred from the normal course of events. Another way of understanding this is to think of the *future event* retroactively affecting our awareness at an earlier time—the future affecting the past. In what follows, I will present some very compelling evidence of this ability—both from the laboratory and from what we like to think of as real life. It's important to remember that psychic abilities were not invented in the lab. They have been found occurring naturally in the field—for millennia.

Ludwig Wittgenstein wrote, "Whereof one cannot speak, thereof one must remain silent."[1] This was an early statement of the "Logical Positivist" view that states that scientists and philosophers cannot meaningfully write about things that can be neither verified nor falsified—such as the idea that chocolate is better than vanilla. Questions like, "Did God create the universe?" or "Is consciousness material or nonmaterial?" can create a lot of hard feelings. But there is no experiment or measurement that will answer them.

Up to this point, I have hewed to this general principal that verification is essential—especially concerning remote viewing. But I am now going to describe data and experiences that challenge our ordinary understanding of time and causality. And the evidence indicates that there is something completely wrong with our understanding of causality. This is a serious problem, because from a physicist's point of view, if you don't understand causality, you don't understand anything!

A physicist might accept that we can experience something that is occurring hundreds of miles away, because it seems a little like "mental radio." Seeing something in the distance by ESP seems causal, like ordinary vision—only more so. Whereas seeing something in the future appears to the physicist as frighteningly acausal. In fact, Einstein even expressed an interest in psychic perception in his preface to Upton Sinclair's book *Mental Radio*.[2] But when we explore our experiences of events *before* they occur, it can create great epistemological resistance.

Physicists believe Newton's first law, which states that force equals mass times acceleration (F = ma). That is, when you push a wagon, its acceleration is proportional to the force of your push. The unspoken assumption is that the movement of the wagon comes after your push, not before it. That's what we usually mean by causality. The event comes *after* the cause— it's about time. However, the data from decades of precognition research show that a plane crash on Thursday can cause a traveler to have a frightening dream on Wednesday night, thereby affecting the traveler's behavior the next day—even before the crash has occurred.

In this regard, it is interesting to note that all four of the aircraft that flew into the Twin Towers, the Pentagon, and the farm field in Pennsylvania on 9/11/2001 were unusually empty. I was at a conference in Assisi, Italy, at the time and have kept the *International Herald Tribune* of September 12, 2001. The story indicated that *each of the four* hijacked planes were surprisingly carrying *less than half* the usual number of morning commute passengers on that fateful day. The load factor for the four planes was only 31 percent. Perhaps *one* unusually empty plane could be explained away—but not all four. There were lots of unclaimed tickets. Apparently, many people just had a gut feeling that this was not a good morning to get on a plane.

Similarly, W. E. Cox (at J. B. Rhine's Duke University laboratory) investigated railroad train wrecks and found that in the 1950s, railroad trains that crashed or derailed on the East Coast had significantly fewer passengers on the day they crashed than the same trains on other days—even taking weather into account.[3] These data provide strong evidence that people can and do use their intuition of the future to save their lives.

Precognitive dreams are probably the most common psychic event to appear in the life of the average person. These dreams give us a glimpse of events that we will experience the next day or in the near future. They occur when one's *present* dreaming consciousness (brain) has an experience that is strongly correlated to a real-world event experienced by one's *future* awake consciousness (brain). Such a correlation could occur through the quantum mechanical entanglement of particles in the central nervous system. The great physicist David Bohn called this "quantum interconnectedness."

In 1926, Erwin Schrödinger discovered the principle of entanglement, or non-separation, of which he said, "I would not call that *one* but rather *the* characteristic trait of quantum mechanics."[4] In 1933, he received a Nobel Prize for his pioneering theoretical work. In October 2022, three physicists—Alain Aspect, John F. Clauser, and Anton Zeilinger—received Nobel Prizes for their experimental demonstration of Schrödinger's ideas.[5]

(In 1972, I had an opportunity to visit John Clauser's impoverished Berkeley laboratory where he was the first to demonstrate Schrödinger's entangled photons, fifty short years before he shared his Nobel Prize for what Reuters headlined as "Sleuths of 'spooky' quantum science win Nobel physics prize." In September 2022, just one month prior, the International Remote Viewing Association (IRVA) celebrated the fiftieth anniversary of remote viewing research at Stanford Research Institute. SRI has lots of good-looking publications in *Nature* and the *Proceedings of the IEEE,* but no Nobel Prize—yet.)

I believe that the precognitive dream is often caused by an experience that we actually will have at a later time. If you have a dream of an elephant passing in front of your window, and wake up the next morning to find a circus parade led by an elephant going down your street (for the first time ever), we would say that last night's dream of an elephant was caused by your experience of seeing the elephant the next morning.

To know that a dream is precognitive, you must learn to recognize that it is not caused by the (a) previous day's mental residue, (b) your wishes, or (c) your anxieties. We find, rather, that precognitive dreams tend to have (a) an unusual clarity and (b) often contain bizarre and unfamiliar material. Dream experts like to speak of their *preternatural* clarity. These are not *wish fulfillment* or *anxiety* dreams.

Ordinary dreams may be of the wish fulfillment variety. Will the girl of my dreams marry me? They can be anxiety dreams. Am I going to fail the exam that I didn't study for? They can be dreams made out of the previous day's residue. In such a dream you might feel frightened about yesterday's experience of your canoe capsizing. Those are all interesting dreams, but they are not precognitive. On the other hand, if you have had hundreds of plane flights and then have a frightening dream about a crash, you might want to rethink your travel plans.

I occasionally have very clear precognitive dreams. For me, a precognitive dream must be bizarre and outside my possible ordinary day's activities. Plus, as mentioned, it must have unusual clarity. To make sure that you are not fooling yourself, you must either write down the dreams that you think are precognitive or you must tell them to someone. If you have a wonderfully clear precognitive dream, but you don't document that you thought it was precognitive before the event occurs, you do not get credit for it in the "Big Book." That is, you want to have confidence that a dream is truly precognitive if you are going to act on it.

Let me tell you about one such dream that I had. I don't write down my dreams, but the dreams I tell my wife about are the ones that I am pretty confident will come to pass in the next day or two. So, I had this dream in which a toy electric train was running all the way around the square base of the ceiling in our cathedral-ceiling living room. I could see the train clearly, like a boxy Märklin train from Germany. It was a nice dream. I do not have any such train, but forty years ago my children had one in another house.

This dream met all five of my requirements. I told my wife about the dream, got my cup of coffee, and took it into my home office. I turned on my computer to my home page, which is the *New York Times*. Any guess as to what the picture was? The big news in the *Times* that day was the repair and rebuilding of The Loop, the elevated train in downtown Chicago, where I grew up and where my father had his book shop. It showed *exactly* the boxy train from my dream, running in the circle of The Loop. It was a total surprise and totally accurate.

Figure 34. Chicago elevated train in The Loop

In the case I describe here, the dreamer's sleeping self (me) appears to be entangled with my wide-awake future self. That future self's experience is the likely source of my precognitive dream. Our research shows conclusively that feedback significantly augments remote viewing, but it is not essential.

Sometimes, I have *failed to report* a dream that did manifest the next day. We call that a type-One error (rejection of a true hypothesis). I have also *told my wife* about some crazy dreams that did *not* come true. That is a type-Two error (the mistaken acceptance of a false hypothesis). Not reporting a potentially false hypothesis is a good choice in the science business, where it is essential to reject nonsense. It is a bad choice in the safety business, where you can tolerate some false alarms, but you cannot tolerate many unreported accidents that are likely to occur.

For example, one of our CIA government contract monitors was in Detroit with his colleague, overseeing another project for which he was responsible. Although they had gotten to bed very late on their last night there, my friend had a hard time getting to sleep. When he finally did fall asleep, he had a frightening dream in which he was in a fiery airplane crash. All through the next day, he was concerned about the dream, since he was scheduled to fly out of Detroit that evening. Because the dream had been so horrifyingly realistic, he ultimately decided to try to avoid having that experience in real life. He told his partner that he was going to stay over in Detroit for another day.

Of course, he thought that it was very unlikely that his plane would actually crash. On the other hand, he had seen enough psychic events in our SRI laboratory to give him pause—and he had an adorable little daughter at home whom he wanted to see again. Since he, like most of us, did not want to appear to be silly or superstitious, he didn't tell his buddy why he was delaying his departure. (And in certain branches of the government, you are taught not to ask too many questions.) Later that day, after delivering his partner to the airport, our friend was driving away along the frontage road and heard a muffled explosion. It was the crash of his airplane, killing many passengers, including his partner. Our friend was in shock for a week.

This is an example of the future affecting the past. There is an enormous body of evidence for this kind of occurrence. So, what can we conclude from this true story? First of all, everyone is probably a little anxious about flying. But I, for one, have never had a dream of being in a crash and neither had my friend. In his business, he was a very frequent flyer—thousands of flights. So, we can postulate, without conducting a survey, that to dream of being in a plane crash is a somewhat unusual event. "But," I hear you saying, "he wasn't in a plane crash. He just witnessed one." This deals with one of the most interesting questions in all of psychic research: Can you use precognitive information to change a future that you perceive but do not like? The problem comes, of course, from the idea that if you change the future so that the unpleasant thing doesn't happen to you, where did the dream come from? There are two fairly sensible answers to that question, both of which might be correct.

A precognitive dream is not a prophecy: it is a forecast, based on all presently available data or world lines. If you view the world as a huge four-dimensional space-time cube, then we can be thought of as moving through the three-dimensional part like Hansel and Gretel trailing bread crumbs. Similarly, we move along the line of time at a rate of one second per second. Thus, our lives *trace a path* through the three spatial dimensions and one time dimension of this great cube comprising all of space and time. That path is known as our individual world line. If I wish to make use of my newly received, precognitively derived information, I can change the future.

For example, if I am looking forward to having a dinner date with someone and have a very clear dream about meeting her in a colorful and unusual restaurant, I will have a certain level of confidence that the event will come to pass—even though it might also be a wish fulfillment dream. However, if I tell my perspective dinner companion about my dream, she may say, "I was planning to meet you at that new and

interesting restaurant, but I don't want you to get the idea that
I am a slave to your dreams, so I'll see you next week instead."

This is the vicious-circle type of paradox about self-
referential statements that Bertrand Russell describes in his
Theory of Types—falsifying the future by using information
from the future. The dream is a forecast of events to come
about in the future unless you do something to change them,
*based upon the dream information. Such an action does not
falsify the forecast.* There is no paradox. To make this clear,
since it is a cause of a lot of confusion, we can discuss another
hypothetical example.

A messenger has information from a spy who has learned
that the enemy is going to attack us. That's the equivalent of a
"precognitive message." Armed with this new data, we launch
a surprise attack on the enemy, and chase him away. He then,
of course, cannot and does not attack us. However, we do not
fire the messenger or the spy because the information in their
message didn't come to pass. Their message described the
probable future, which would have come to pass without the
intervention that was made possible by the message.

A second question is, "How can I dream about being in a
plane crash if I don't actually experience it?" The answer here
is quite different. You dream about the real crash, then drama-
tize the events to include yourself in it. Our friend saw a plane
crash at quite close range, and since he was supposed to be on
the plane, he had no trouble putting himself on the plane in
his dream. We would say that the frightening crash that he
witnessed the following afternoon was the cause of his dream
the previous night.

This is called retro-causality, and it may be the basis of
most precognition. It is important to realize and understand

that a future event does not have to be directly perceived or experienced to have a retro-causal effect or give rise to precognitive awareness. Studies in 1964 by Gertrude Schmeidler at City College of New York showed significant precognition in forced-choice trials (that is, those in which one knows the range of possible targets) using computer-generated targets *and the viewers did not receive any feedback.*[6]

However, what cannot happen, I believe, is a future event changing the past. It is certain that nothing in the future can cause something that has already happened to have *not* happened. This is what philosophers call the *intervention paradox,* illustrated by the thought experiment in which you kill your grandmother when she was a child, and you therefore cannot exist—or worse, cease to exist. That kind of thing is interesting to think about, but there is not a drop of evidence to make us believe that this type of contradiction can occur. The Persian poet/astronomer Omar Khayyam described the immutability of past events beautifully in the famous lines of his timeless epic, *The Rubaiyat,* around 1100 CE.

> *The moving Finger writes; and, having writ,*
> *Moves on: nor all your Piety nor Wit,*
> *Shall lure it back to cancel half a Line,*
> *Nor all your Tears wash out a Word of it.*

In all of this, we are arguing against the existence of any implacable arrow of time. Rather, we would say that there are certain time-irreversible phenomena, such as heat conduction, diffusion, chemical reactions, and alas, aging. In all of these cases, a movie of the effect under consideration will quickly reveal whether it is being run forward or backward. On the other hand, there are a wide variety of reversible effects that can be run either way. These include all of electro-magnetism, radio wave propagation, and the laws of mechanics when there is no friction. Paradoxically, there is no time for a swinging pendulum. So, it appears that the irreversibility of time is more *fact-like* than *law-like*. It all depends on the type of event being observed. There is obviously *no law against precognition,* and under the right conditions, it is a common occurrence at the atomic and subatomic level.

From 1935 to 1989, in an exhaustive summary of research data of paranormal foreknowledge of the future, Charles Honorton and Diane Ferrari found that 309 precognition experiments had been carried out by sixty-two investigators.[7] More than fifty thousand participants were involved in more than two million trials. They reported that 30 percent of these studies were statistically significant in showing that people can describe future events, where only 5 percent would be expected by chance. This gave an overall significance of greater than 10^{20} (more than a billion billion) to one, which is akin to throwing seventy pennies in the air and having every one come down heads. This body of data offers very strong evidence for confirming the existence of foreknowledge of the future—it cannot just be ascribed to somebody's lucky day—and clearly shows that we misunderstand our relationship to the dimension of time.

For years, parapsychologists have been trying to find ways to encourage their subjects to demonstrate psychic glimpses of the future. These 309 experiments were forced-choice experiments, in which subjects had to choose which of four colored buttons was about to be illuminated or which one of five cards they would be shown at a later time. In all of these cases, a random number generator of some sort selected the targets, to which the researchers were blind. Participants had to try to guess what they would be shown in the future from among known alternatives.

In some cases, as in the 1964 trials, they had to indicate which target would be randomly chosen in the future, and they *never received any feedback at all* about what target was actually selected. We can glean two pieces of important information from these studies: there is overwhelming evidence for the existence of precognition, and there are more successful and less successful ways to do experiments.

Four different factors were found to significantly vary the success or failure of the trials. It is important to keep these ingredients in mind if you want your own experiments to succeed. First, experiments are much more successful when they are carried out with subjects who are experienced and interested in the outcome, rather than people who are inexperienced and uninterested. For example, running ESP trials in a classroom of moderately bored students will rarely show any kind of success, but researchers keep doing it nonetheless. Furthermore, participants who are enthusiastic about the experiment are usually the most successful at precognition. The difference in scoring rate between experienced and inexperienced subjects was significant at 1,000 to 1 against chance.

Another factor shows that tests with *individual* percipients were much more successful than experiments with groups. Making the trials meaningful to each participant is important to success. The success level comparing individuals versus groups was statistically significant at 30 to 1 against chance.

Third, feedback is valuable. I have always found that feedback is very helpful to all psi functioning. In precognition, I feel that it is the *experience* the viewer has when shown the feedback at a later time that is often (but not always) the source of the precognitive experience. This view is strongly supported by the forced-choice studies.

Finally, the data show that the sooner the participants get the feedback, the greater the hit rate. That is, it appears that for forced-choice targets, it is easier to foretell the immediate future than the distant future. In laboratory experiments, people did very well in predicting events seconds or minutes in advance, but did less well looking hours or days in advance. This seems to be the case for naturally occurring precognition as well. On the other hand, it is also possible that people tend to forget dreams of far future events before they have a chance to be corroborated.

Thus, the four factors that are important in these studies are:

1. Practiced (talented) vs. inexperienced subjects
2. Individual vs. group testing
3. Feedback vs. no feedback
4. Short time interval between subject response and target generation
5. Here I would add a *fifth* point: Free-response experiments, such as remote viewing, are much more successful than forced-choice experiments, for all the reasons we have been discussing. Forced-choice

experiments encourage guessing and naming, which is always a bad idea.

In the whole database of the Honorton-Ferrari analysis, there were some experiments that had all four favorable factors and some that had all four unfavorable factors. After all is said and done, 87.5 percent of the psi-conducive, favorable studies were successful and significant, while *none* of the totally unfavorable studies were statistically significant. Since we now routinely carry out experiments under the favorable conditions, I think that we can say that we have learned something about psi in the past fifty years. Actually, we have learned quite a lot.

We know for example, that a forced-choice ESP test is a very inefficient way to elicit psi functioning. In the above studies, the experimenters, on average, had to carry out 3,600 trials to achieve a statistically significant result. With the free-response type of experiment, such as remote viewing, we typically have to do only six to nine trials. In the case of our precognition experiments with Hella—which we published in the *Proceedings of the IEEE*—we had a total of four targets, all of which she described correctly.

We are all familiar with the idea of a premonition, in which one has inner knowledge of something that is going to happen in the future—usually something bad! There is also an experience called *presentiment,* in which one has an inner sensation, a gut feeling that something strange is about to occur. An example would be for you to suddenly stop on your walk down the street because you felt "uneasy," only to have a flower pot fall off a window ledge and land at your feet instead of on your head. That would be a useful presentiment.

I recently had a useful presentiment. One Friday evening, I was quietly paying bills at my desk when I began to worry obsessively about what would happen if I lost my credit card. (I had never previously lost a credit card.) So strong was this fear that I stopped what I was doing and went to the next room to get my credit card from my wallet and compulsively wrote its numbers in my personal telephone book.

The next day I went to a craft fair covering many blocks of University Avenue, the main street of Palo Alto. While there, I bought some beautiful blue ceramic bowls. It was a very hot day and a concessionaire was selling cold beer in celebratory beer mugs. Alas, I had spent all my cash. So I went to an ATM in the wall of a nearby bank building, with my credit card in hand, to obtain some beer money. With cash in one hand and a long colorful receipt in the other, I set off to get my treat to deal with the heat.

Two days later, while trying to pay for my groceries, I discovered with a shock that my credit card was missing from my wallet. After some thought, I was able to deduce that I had probably left it in the ATM at the street fair. But, because of my presentiment, I had the card numbers written down, allowing me to call the card company and ask them to send me a new card. That's the reward for paying attention to your presentiments! Since then, I have memorized my numbers.

In the laboratory, we know that if we show a frightening picture to a person, there will be a significant change in his or her physiology. Their blood pressure, heart rate, and electrical skin resistance will change. This fight-or-flight reaction is called an "orienting response." Researcher Dean Radin has shown at the University of Nevada that this orienting response is also observed in a person's physiology a few seconds *before* they see the scary picture.[8] In balanced, double-blind experiments, Radin has demonstrated that if you are about to see scenes of sexuality, violence, or mayhem, your body will steel itself against the shock or insult. But if you are about to see a picture of a flower garden, then there is no such strong anticipatory reaction. Fear is much easier to measure physiologically than bliss.

The pictures that Radin uses in his experiments are from a standardized and quantified set of emotional stimuli used in psychology research. These range from nudes on the beach and downhill skiing on the positive side, to car crashes and abdominal surgery, generally considered to have negative effect. Pictures of paper cups and fountain pens are found in the neutral range.

The exciting results he has reported is that the higher the emotional score of the picture shown to the subject at a *later* time, the greater in magnitude is the subject's pre-stimulus response before the picture is seen. That is, the numerical score of the picture (the published intensity of the card's impact) actually correlates to the numerical score of the subject at odds greater than 100 to 1. It is this correlation that shows that the effect is real. Professor Dick Bierman at Utrecht University in Holland has successfully replicated Radin's findings. However, he had to assemble a much more "extreme" or explicit set of pictures to psychically excite his blasé Amsterdam college students.

So here is a case in which your direct physical perception of the picture, when it occurs, causes you to have a unique physical response at an earlier time. Your future is affecting your past. William Braud, in his excellent book *Distant Mental Influence,* describes these experiments as follows:

> Although this presentiment effect is usually taken to reflect precognition (future-knowing) operating at an unconscious body level, these interesting findings can just as well be interpreted as instances in which objective events (the presentation of the slide itself or the person's future reaction to the slide) may be acting backward in time to influence the person's physiology.[9]

Even stronger results have been obtained by physicists Edwin May and James Spottiswoode, who measure galvanic skin responses of subjects who are about to hear a loud noise in earphones. Again, measurements show that their nervous system seems to know in advance when it will be assaulted by a disagreeable stimulus. Yet the most significant evidence for this so-called pre-stimulus response comes from the Hungarian researcher Zoltán Vassy. He administers painful electric shocks as the stimulus to be precognized. His results are the strongest of all because the human body does not ever habituate to electric shocks. They are always experienced as a new and alarming stimulus, even though the shock resides in your future.[10] Whereas, after I heard a few loud noise stimuli in May's experiment, my body quickly realized that the noise was not actually going to hurt me, so I became much more meditative than vigilant—causing a decline in the pre-stimulus response. This may be unique to me, because I am both a researcher and an experienced meditator.

Daryl Bem is a very quick and imaginative psychology professor at Cornell University. He is also an accomplished practitioner of magic. I am happy to consider him a good friend, and over the decades I have enjoyed his company. After several years of comfortable tenure doing perceptual psychology at Cornell University, Prof. Bem began devoting himself to a detailed study of precognition and premonition in the laboratory. He is deeply inquisitive and has an almost unlimited supply of undergraduate students to act as subjects for his experiments.

Over a period of several years, Bem carried out nine formal experimental series to examine how our present feelings and choices are affected by things that happen to us *at a later time*. For example, a man deciding which of two sisters to marry might have the feeling that although one potential bride, Sue, is much prettier than her sister, in his gut he can already feel that the other, Sarah, will make him happier in the future. We might chalk this up to good judgment. Or we could say that it is the future calling to him. Bem showed us how to find out which was the case.[11]

All nine of Bem's experiments involved one hundred to two hundred college students who each had to make a choice of which one of two video screens to select, based on something they would see at a later time. The students were not aware of this future component. Sometimes they would be subliminally precognitive about getting what they *wanted* in the future. However, sometimes the images requiring them to be psychic were about avoiding what they *didn't want* to have happen.

In Bem's first experiment, secretly called "Detect Erotic," students were asked to volunteer for an ESP experiment for which they would be paid or would receive a unit of college credit. The students thought this was a familiar type of ESP experiment in which one has to press a button to indicate which of two screens would show a picture. One screen would offer an interesting color picture, while the other screen would remain blank. That's what they expected, and that's what it looked like.

In reality, there were three *types* of pictures available—erotic, neutral, or negative. We all know what erotic pictures are. Neutral pictures are things like flowers and coffee cups. Negative pictures can be car crashes, surgery, some form of violence, etc. What the students didn't know was that the screen chosen to display the picture would be randomly decided *after* they had made their selection. *And* that the choice of which of three types of photo would also be randomly chosen after their button press. Thus, at the time of their button press, neither the picture nor its location had been determined.

The not-too-surprising result showed that undergraduate college students were more successful at finding the location of the erotic stimuli than they were at finding coffee cups or car crashes. In fact, the random erotic stimuli were correctly located significantly more often than either of the other pictures—statistically significant at odds of 100 to 1. Interestingly, the students who were rated as "extroverted," found the erotic picture 57 percent of the time—at odds of almost 1 in 10,000. Extroverts almost always seem do better in ESP tests.

I will describe one other of Bem's experiments—this one about *avoidance*. In this case, there were also one hundred students, but the task didn't even look like an ESP test. Each subject had thirty-two trials in which they briefly (thirty-three milliseconds) saw a pair of neutral pictures—each was the mirror image of the other. The student's task was simply to press a key indicating, "the picture you like better." The "correct" target picture was then determined by a random number generator, after the student's choice. If the student preferred the "incorrect" picture, they were next shown "a highly arousing *negative* picture." This was flashed three times for thirty-three milliseconds each time.

The students were highly successful in avoiding the negative pictures, by previously choosing the "correct" picture, at odds of 7 in 1,000. Again, the extroverts were more than twice as successful—avoiding the nasty pictures at odds of 2 in 1,000 ($P = 0.002$). Bem carried out seven other variations on this theme.

Two trials involved what he calls *retroactive priming*. That is, he gave his subject a clue to the right answer, subliminally, *after* they had made a choice. We know that subliminal information or pictures in the movie theater can interest you in buying popcorn or Coke. In these experiments, Bem asked the subjects to express their feelings about pictures that they briefly viewed—expressing their opinion as to whether a picture was pleasant or unpleasant. *After* they made their choice, the students saw the word "beautiful" or "ugly."

Experiment	Number of Trials	Probability
Detect Erotic	100	.01
Avoid Negative	150	.009
Retro Priming I	97	.007
Retro Priming II	99	.014
Retro Habituation I	100	.014
Retro Habituation II	150	.009
Retro Boredom	200	.096
Retro Recall I	100	.029
Retro Recall II	50	.002

Table 3: Summary of Daryl Bem's nine precognition experiments (statistical significance for the nine experimental series is 6.6 standard deviations from chance; P = 1.34 x 10^{-11})

In both of these experiments, the students' opinions were significantly colored by the words flashed *after* they had made their choices. The simple description of all these experiments is that they are demonstrations of how the future affects the past. Bem's overall significance for this series of experiments is more than *1,000,000,000 to 1*. I show the summary results of his experimental series in Table 3.

Bem's sixty-page paper documents his hugely significant accomplishment and shows that the future can not only be known and felt—which is why he called his paper "Feeling the Future"—but, more than that, can be replicated with great success over a long period of time. This paper is one in a family of research approaches that show that psi is not weak nor is it illusive—a very important finding.

CHAPTER 8

Learning How to Do Remote Viewing

O ne might ask, in the SRI program of remote viewing–generated information, if there was ever sufficient significance to influence decisions at a policy level. This is, of course, impossible to determine unless policymakers were to come forward with a statement to the affirmative. One example of a possible candidate for policy change is a study we performed at SRI during the Carter-administration debates concerning the proposed deployment of the mobile MX Missile System. In that scenario, to avoid detection, missiles were to be randomly shuffled from silo to silo in a silo field—a sort of high-tech shell game.

In a computer simulation of a twenty-silo field with randomly assigned (hidden) missile locations, we were able—using information generated by Associative Remote Viewing (ARV), like the silver futures forecasting (described in chapter 9)—to show rather forcefully that the application of a sophisticated statistical-averaging technique could, in principle, permit an adversary to defeat the system.

Hal Puthoff briefed the appropriate offices on these results at their request, and a written report with the technical details was widely circulated among groups responsible for threat analysis. What role, if any, our contribution played in the mix of factors behind the enormously complex decision to cancel the program will probably never be known and was likely negligible. Nonetheless, this is a prototypical example of the kind of tasking we did at SRI, which, by its nature, had potential policy implications.[1] In plain English, it is my understanding that our demonstration of the ability to psychically locate their simulated hidden MX missiles scared the hell out of the Office of Technology Assessment. Ingo Swann was the remote viewer, and three months later, the silo shell game–program was killed.

As you can see, there are many and varied application for this technique. In this chapter, I will describe the very simple first steps you can take toward learning remote viewing. This skill is a two-person game, especially in the beginning. You, the viewer, will describe your mental impressions of the interesting little target object that your friend, the interviewer, has brought to you for a learning session. Your interviewer should have a collection of such interesting little objects and have put each of them into its own small brown-paper bag.

Now there is a very tricky protocol decision to make before you start. When I teach remote viewing, I always like the first two trials to include the possibility of a telepathic—mind-to-mind—channel between the interviewer and the viewer. This gives the viewer three possible paths for receiving psychic data. There is the telepathic connection with your *friend,* who already knows the answer. There is the direct clairvoyant connection to the *target object.* And there is the *precognitive* channel from the *feedback* you will receive *after* you have finished your viewing—when your friend puts the object into your hand in the future.

However, if your interviewer knows the target, there is always a possibility of getting subconscious cues as to the correctness of what you say or draw as you go along in a session. This would be a very bad outcome. In this case, you would only be learning to read your friend's breathing and tone of voice, and nothing about your own psychic and mental processes.

Interestingly, if we go to the experts, we learn that Ingo Swann thinks that the early stages of remote viewing can be well advanced by an interviewer who knows the answer. He argued this when he taught the military at SRI. On the other hand, Joe McMoneagle says in his book *Remote Viewing Secrets* that "all persons present should be blind to the target."[2] So, what to do?

In 2010, I was in Paris attending the international meeting of the Parapsychological Association, where I received an Outstanding Career award. At this meeting, I spoke to skeptically oriented researchers. I told them how easy and natural psychic functioning is to elicit from interested participants— quite different from what many of them had experienced.

At the end of my talk, a young woman researcher asked me if I could show her how it worked. The next day, she and her colleague took my wife and me to Chartres Cathedral, a site we both had longed to visit. Later in the afternoon at a café, I told our delightful new friend Claire that I had brought something for her to psychically view and describe. This, of course, was not a double-blind experiment, but she obviously had no idea what I had brought from America for this informal trial.

I am experienced enough that I am confident I didn't subconsciously whisper the answer to her. I simply turned over a paper placemat, gave her a pen, and said the magic words: "I have an interesting little object that I have brought for you to view. Please tell me about the surprising images that appear in your awareness. I have an object that needs a description. Don't try to name it or guess what it is. Just tell me about your new and surprising impressions."

Her responses are shown in Figure 35. The target had three components. It was a silver-plated, collapsible drinking cup with a little handle that folds up inside the cup. Because this cup is part of another experiment that I carry out in workshops, it happened to have a silver dollar in the bottom. Additionally, the cup resides in a cylindrical, alligator-skin box with a tight-fitting lid. I consider this to be a difficult and complex target, and I told that to Claire in advance.

The first thing Claire drew was a little circle on the left of the paper. She said, "I see something round and flat." I didn't comment, but instead suggested that we take a little break to see if something else would come into her awareness. (I had completely forgotten about the silver dollar in the cup.)

After the break, Claire said, "I see a shiny metal cylinder. It goes up and down!" She drew this, then we took another little break. Finally she made a third drawing of a cross-hatched little cylinder that she said was also part of the target. So there it was, a representation of the silver dollar on the left, the cup in the center, and the alligator-skin box on the right. This whole

Figure 35. Collapsible silver cup target and drawings of remote viewer at a café in France

process, the remarkably accurate description of an absurdly complicated target, took about ten minutes.

My first rule for learning remote viewing is that *remote viewing should be fun!* I believe that the mind-to-mind channel I just described can work so excellently that it would be a pity to deprive yourself of the experience, especially in the early stages of learning remote viewing and dealing with mental images. However, after a couple of such trials, I believe you should work in a double-blind situation.

You can do this by having the interviewer thoroughly mix up the bags that hold each object, so that no one can know what any one particular bag holds. Then take one of the bags and put it on the floor, out of sight. In fact, all the bags should be kept out of sight because people will tend to stare at the bags—as though seeing into them with x-ray vision like Superman. That is not the way remote viewing works.

You are then ready to go for a double-blind trial. In the remote viewing experiments and operational trials at SRI,

I *never* knew the target. All experiments were double-blind from the beginning.

Your friend should sit with you in a dimly lit room, each of you with pen and paper, and tell you that there is "an object that needs a description." If you come into the session with clearly formed initial impressions or images, it is very important that you write them down on the top of the paper and label them "initial images." Otherwise, they will follow you all through your session. Draw a line under them to separate them from the rest of the transcript, recognizing that they may or may not have anything to do with the day's target.

Close your eyes, relax for a little while, and tell your friend about all your *mental pictures* relating to the object, *starting with the very first fragmentary shapes or forms.* These first psychic bits are the most important shapes that you will see. Make little sketches of these images as they come to view, even if they don't make sense or are not really objects. "Naming" and analyzing are the principal enemies of remote viewing. Your hand may make little movements in the air over the paper. Notice them and describe what your subliminal mind is trying to tell you.

Good. Now take a break. Remember to breathe after each new picture comes into view. You should then look again at your internal mental slate. In this second look, hopefully you will "see" or be given another, different bit (image), but you may see the same one again. As a viewer, you are *looking for particularly surprising and novel images that do not belong to your normal repertoire of mental images.*

Take another break. For the third viewing, imagine you are holding the object in your hand. Ask yourself questions, such as: Does it have a color or texture? Is it shiny? Does it have sharp edges? What could I do with it? Does it have movable parts? Does it have an odor? Is it heavy or light, wood or metal? Write down your answers, based on your feelings and mental pictures. You should continue this process until no new images or pieces of information come to you. Ingo Swann called this third phase, "sensing the aesthetic impact."

The whole process should not take more than ten to fifteen minutes. Remember . . . to be right, you have to be willing to be wrong. This is where the issue of trust between the two remote viewing partners is so important. The good news is that through this process, you can learn to give a surprisingly coherent description of a hidden object. The bad news is that you are exceedingly unlikely ever to know *psychically* exactly what the object is—because that kind of knowing requires analysis and naming.

After you have described a number of different images, it is a good practice to make a summary of all the things you have said. Try to specify which images you feel the most strongly about versus the ones that are more likely noise from memory or imagination or things you saw earlier in the day. That is, you must go through your notes and try to separate out your most confident psychic bits from the analytical noise. The remaining collection of bits will be your final description of the target. Historically, ESP researchers have found that these "confidence calls" are often the best indication of correctness.

If, however, you had been told in advance that your target would be one of two or more specific objects that had been *named* for you, it would greatly increase the difficulty of describing the correct target, since you would have a clear mental picture of the items in your mind. To separate out the psychic bits of information from the analytic overlay (mental noise), you may have to go through the bit-collecting process many times. Therefore, we strongly recommend that *you don't work with targets known to you.*

To the best of my knowledge, Ingo Swann was the only person who could reliably discriminate between known targets. He was right 80 percent of the time, for example, in formal SRI experiments (comprising fifty trials) in which he had to differentiate between two types of graph paper—cross-section paper and polar-coordinate paper!

After you have made your sketches and written down your impressions, your friend should show you the object. Your interviewer should go over with you all the correct things you saw in your description and point out the things you missed. You can then have the experience of saying, "I saw one of those, but I didn't mention it!" However, the rule in the remote viewing game is that *if it didn't get down on the paper, it didn't happen.* Consequently, it is important to write down or draw *everything;* eventually you will learn to separate the signal from the noise.

We often say that psi is like a musical ability. It is widely distributed in the population, and everyone has some ability and can participate to some extent. Even the most nonmusical person can learn to play a little Mozart on the piano. On the other hand, there is no substitute for innate talent and practice. If all this sounds very simple, it is. I'm simply telling you how to get started and, most importantly, give you permission to express and use your innate abilities and gifts. From three decades of experience, I have no doubt that you can do remote viewing if you follow these instructions. No secret ingredient has been omitted. I wish you success and the feelings of excitement and awe that accompany it.

After you have demonstrated for yourself that these intuitive abilities are indeed available, you may begin to wonder about other aspects of your nonlocal mind that can be explored. The true value of remote viewing lies in the fact that it puts us in contact with the part of our consciousness that is clearly unbounded by distance or time. Remote viewing allows us to become aware of our universal connection to one another and our interdependent nature. Its importance becomes particularly apparent when we share our knowledge with our friends. I believe that we are here to help one another expand our awareness and to enable one another to come in contact with our greater spiritual community.

Astronomers are now able to receive and analyze signals from radio stars that are billions of miles from earth. Masers (microwave amplification by stimulated emission of radiation—like lasers but with an "m") are able to amplify the signal without adding noticeably to the background stellar noise in which it is buried. However, to make this work, the detection system must be operated at greatly reduced temperatures, since the instruments at normal room temperature create their own noise and drown out the extremely weak millimeter-wave signals.

The important factor in detecting weak signals is finding a way to increase the ratio of the signal to the noise. If the incoming signal has an energy of ten microwatts and the ambient noise is also ten microwatts, the signal-to-noise ratio is one—ten divided by ten—which is a very difficult situation for detection. If we can chill down the entire detection system, and reduce the noise from ten microwatts to one, we will have increased the signal-to-noise ratio by a factor of ten. Then we can find something.

We do not know how to increase the psychic signal that appears in our awareness. Instead, we have become very skillful at reducing the mental noise. In laboratory remote viewing, we work with interesting but unknown targets instead of numbers and letters. Removing numbers and letters as targets is one way of reducing the mental noise.

Once, when I was teaching in Italy at the lakeside town of Arco, an architect was one of the remote viewers, and his target picture was the Parthenon. He created a detailed drawing of a classical building in "blueprint" view—in which the columns of the temple had all been laid out flat, their locations indicated by dots inside a main rectangle. This kind of dynamic activity is often seen in remote viewing pictures. Fragmentation is common when a target has repeated elements, such as the stars and stripes of an American flag, a row of columns, or a string of beads.

Ingo Swann devoted a chapter to this kind of distortion in his excellent book *Natural ESP*.[3] He called it "lack of fusion" and gave four degrees of distortion:

1. All parts are *correctly* perceived, but will not connect to form a whole.
2. Some parts are fused, others are not.
3. Fusion is only approximate.

4. Parts are incorrectly fused; all parts are there, but put together in such a way as to falsely create another image.

René Warcollier, a French engineer, also described this phenomenon in his 1948 ground-breaking book *Mind to Mind*. Warcollier called this "parallelism," where similar geometric elements rearrange themselves.

What seems to happen in the case of geometric figures is that movement is injected into what would otherwise be a static image. . . . It is almost as if we had for telepathy *no memory trace* of specific geometric figures, such as the rectangle and the circle. Instead we possess only angles and arcs. . . . There is a sort of mutual attraction between suitable parts, a kind of grouping which I call "the law of parallelism."[4]

From his hundreds of picture-drawing trials, Warcollier gave half a dozen illustrations of this *parallelism,* or *lack of fusion defect.* These are shown in Figure 36, where symbols are broken into angles and arcs.

Warcollier had great insight into the psychic perception problem. He, and later Ingo Swann, taught that mental analysis, memory, and imagination constitute a kind of mental noise in the remote viewing channel. Therefore, the closer the viewer can get to raw, uninterpreted imagery and experience, the better. He or she should be encouraged to report spontaneous perceptions (What are you experiencing now? What

Figure 36. René Warcollier's experiments demonstrating lack of fusion

are you seeing that makes you say such and such?) rather than analysis, since the naked direct experience tends to be "on target," while the analysis is usually incorrect.

Warcollier also presents both theory and experiments of psi communication in *Mind to Mind*. He describes in detail why free-response experiments are almost always greatly superior to forced-choice trials, because they free the viewer from the mental noise of memory and imagination. Unfortunately, it took many years for ESP researchers to take the ideas of this brilliant observer into account when designing their experiments.

In fact, when we were first starting out, Sid Gottlieb (head of the CIA's Project MKUltra) tried to get us to go in a very different direction. Hal Puthoff and I first met him in his basement office at the CIA. He was sitting at his desk, smoking a pipe, surrounded on all sides by a vast collection of books from Buddhism to chemistry. He seemed an amiable man, and we tried to forget that he had spent the past decade torturing people all over the world to get information for the CIA. Sid and I spent more that an hour talking about the psychedelics that we had loved and those we didn't. He strongly suggested that we give LSD to our remote viewing subjects to help them to become more forthcoming!

I told him that it would certainly make them more talkative, but in remote viewing it is very important that the viewer remain as discerning and vigilant as possible so as to separate the psychic signal from the mental noise. Remote viewing is not some kind of trip.

However, remaining "discerning and vigilant" does not mean "analyzing." One of the most important things that we have learned in remote viewing research is that analysis of target possibilities is the enemy of psi. If your only criterion for the existence of psi is how accurately a person can psychically read the serial number on your dollar bill or other such analytic information, then you'll conclude that there is no psychic functioning.

This concept was understood by the famous "muckraker" and writer Upton Sinclair, who, in his 1930 book *Mental Radio*,[5] thoughtfully describes years of successful telepathic picture-drawing experiments that he carried out with his wife Mary Craig.

Craig was a heartful and spiritual woman who had a deep understanding, both intuitive and analytical, of the process of psychic perception. The following paragraphs contain her instructions, condensed from a lengthy chapter in *Mental Radio*. They are reprinted here because her work demonstrates that she had mastered the art of mind-to-mind connection. In describing her technique for "the art of conscious mind-reading," she says:

> The first thing you have to do is learn the trick of undivided attention, or concentration . . . putting the attention on *one* object. . . . It isn't thinking; it is inhibiting thought. . . .
>
> You have to inhibit the impulse to think things about the object, to examine it, or appraise it, or to allow memory-trains to attach themselves to it. . . . Simultaneously, [you] must learn to relax, for strangely enough, a part of concentration is complete relaxation . . . under specified control. . . .
>
> Also, there is something else to it—the power of supervising the condition. You succeed presently in establishing a blank state of consciousness, yet you have the power to become instantly conscious. . . . Also, you control, to a certain degree, what is to be presented to consciousness when you are ready to become conscious.[6]

In *Mental Radio*, Sinclair presents more than one hundred fifty picture-drawing experiments that he and his wife had carried out. As she described above, she developed great skill and insight into perfecting her technique for dealing with her mental images. Figure 37 shows eight representative picture pairs from Sinclair's ground-breaking book.

In an earlier chapter, I mentioned that Einstein had commented favorably on Sinclair's experiments in his preface to *Mental Radio*. Einstein and Sinclair both lived in Princeton, New Jersey, at the time of these experiments. Einstein had an opportunity to witness some of them. In his preface he wrote:

> The results of the telepathic experiments carefully and plainly set forth in this book stand surely far beyond those which a nature investigator holds to be thinkable. On the other hand, it is out of the question in the case of so conscientious an observer and writer as Upton Sinclair that he is carrying out a conscious deception on the reading world; his good faith and dependability are not to be doubted.[7]

Remote viewing is a safe and very exhilarating activity that you can learn and practice at home with no fear of bad or frightening experiences. Other practices, however, can be a little more "dangerous." Since the publication of Robert Monroe's book, *Journeys Out of the Body*,[8] people have been asking me about the relationship between remote viewing and out-of-body experiences (OBEs). Here is a brief summary.

In a remote viewing experience, you quiet your mind and describe the images that appear in your awareness—on your

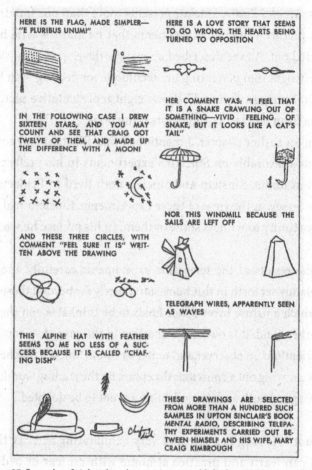

HERE IS THE FLAG, MADE SIMPLER— "E PLURIBUS UNUM!"

HERE IS A LOVE STORY THAT SEEMS TO GO WRONG, THE HEARTS BEING TURNED TO OPPOSITION

IN THE FOLLOWING CASE I DREW SIXTEEN STARS, AND YOU MAY COUNT AND SEE THAT CRAIG GOT TWELVE OF THEM, AND MADE UP THE DIFFERENCE WITH A MOON!

HER COMMENT WAS: "I FEEL THAT IT IS A SNAKE CRAWLING OUT OF SOMETHING—VIVID FEELING OF SNAKE, BUT IT LOOKS LIKE A CAT'S TAIL"

NOR THIS WINDMILL BECAUSE THE SAILS ARE LEFT OFF

AND THESE THREE CIRCLES, WITH COMMENT "FEEL SURE IT IS" WRITTEN ABOVE THE DRAWING

TELEGRAPH WIRES, APPARENTLY SEEN AS WAVES

THIS ALPINE HAT WITH FEATHER SEEMS TO ME NO LESS OF A SUCCESS BECAUSE IT IS CALLED "CHAFING DISH"

THESE DRAWINGS ARE SELECTED FROM MORE THAN A HUNDRED SUCH SAMPLES IN UPTON SINCLAIR'S BOOK *MENTAL RADIO*, DESCRIBING TELEPATHY EXPERIMENTS CARRIED OUT BETWEEN HIMSELF AND HIS WIFE, MARY CRAIG KIMBROUGH

Figure 37. Examples of eight telepathy experiments published in 1930 by Upton Sinclair

mental screen—in response to the suggestions of the interviewer, such as, "I have a target or a hidden object that needs a description." You can describe and experience the color, shape, form, or weight of the object, or the overall architectural appearance of a target location. You can even go inside a distant building. But that's where it begins to merge with out-of-body territory.

Basically, there is a *continuum* from remote viewing to a full out-of-body experience, with no discrete break between one and the other. In an out-of-body experience, you generally start with a simple remote viewing, and then bring along with you your emotionality, sensitivity, and sexuality—to whatever degree you are comfortable. Unlike remote viewing, you definitely have the opportunity to scare yourself in an OBE because of the significant emotional commitment. In an OBE, you can change your point of view of the distant target. You can also have a significant emotional interaction with a person at the target. (Bob Monroe describes such an interaction as leading up to his eventual marriage to the woman he was psychically visiting in an out-of-body journey.)

From my personal experience, OBEs are much more realistic, lifelike, and cinematic than the more diaphanous flickering in and out of most remote viewing experiences. The OBE has a much higher (more detailed) data rate and is much more involving. Nevertheless, as a remote viewer becomes more experienced, their perception also becomes increasingly stable.

I find that OBEs have a similar feeling to lucid dreams, where you find that you are awake in a dream. Once you learn to have and recognize lucid dreams, you will never be overtaken by a nightmare because you will be able to be an active participant in the dream. Dr. Stephen LaBerge from Stanford University received his PhD for his investigation into lucid dreaming and has been teaching the subject since the early 2000s.

My wife, Patty, and I took part in a ten-day "Dream Vacation" on the big island of Hawaii with LaBerge, where we learned to have lucid dreams. After a week of practice, I had an exhilarating flying dream in which I successfully flew out of my room and over the dark craggy bay and sparkly moonlit ocean next to the retreat center where we were staying. I also fulfilled my objective for the trip, which was to learn to control my occasional frightening nightmares, which I have not had since his workshop. However, it is important to remember that a lucid dream is not an OBE. What you see in the dream does not necessarily (or usually) exist.

The great Dzogchen Buddhist teacher, Namkhai Narbu, teaches in his little workbook, *Dream Yoga and the Practice of Natural Light*,[9] that gaining control of your dreams prepares you for your journey through the *bardos*—the period between lives where you have to deal with peaceful or rather terrifyingly wrathful deities. In my view, Dzogchen Buddhism is unquestionably the fast track to freedom, truth, and self-liberation.

We did not teach any of this at SRI. We didn't want anyone to have a bad experience and complain to the management—or the government—that we had separated their consciousness from their body and they were unable to put themselves properly back together again.

People also report powerful and quite realistic sexual experiences during an OBE, including transgender ones. You might have the surprising sensation of being a lover of *either* gender. You may react physically or it may only manifest as an energetic encounter. Ingo Swann calls this "sexuality clairvoyance" and describes this "sexual vibe as a combination of

clairvoyance and telesthesia . . . involving a transfer of sensa-
tions." Swann's book *Psychic Sexuality*[10] is all about sex and psi
on the astral plane. Ingo explains that an inquisitive person
who is unconditionally open to their psychic nature will also
have the opportunity to explore a variety of nonlocal sexual
experiences. However, these loving interactions must between
consenting adults; otherwise it would be a kind of psychic
rape. Swann calls this *telestheia,* a heart-to-heart connection,
as contrasted with *telepathy,* which is a mind-to-mind connection. I have found that sex and psi are natural companions.
The fact that both are repressed in Western society is a cause
for a lot of unnecessary suffering.

A volume for the truly adventurous is *The Confessions of
Aleister Crowley,*[11] in which this audacious magician writes
about his experiences of astral travel, often initiated using sex,
drugs, and ESP. The classic teaching manual on the subject is
The Projection of the Astral Body,[12] by Sylvan Muldoon and
Hereward Carrington. I recommend this 1929 monograph
by a psychic traveler and a scientist, respectively, to get an
early perspective and good instruction on how to start having OBEs. I can personally attest to most of the above experiences, under totally satisfactory *double blind* conditions.
Since mental telepathy is well known to function quite independent of distance, none of these opportunities should be at
all surprising.

McKinley Kantor, Pulitzer prize–winning author of a Civil
War tale called *Andersonville,* also wrote an OBE novel called
Don't Touch Me.[13] When I read *Don't Touch Me,* I came to
believe that it was not entirely fiction but based at least partly
on his personal experiences during the Korean war.

In the novel, he chronicles the trans-Pacific love-making of a soldier with his passionate sweetheart who was living in the States. The girl desperately loved her boyfriend, Wolf, but the time difference made the long-distance relationship very problematic. However, there are very powerful psychic forces acting to pull the separated lovers together. Since everything else Kantor had written was very authentic, why not this first-person narrative.

One evening, I sat with McKinley Kantor at the party celebrating his Pulitzer win for *Andersonville*. He was with his very pregnant wife, and they were happy to confirm that his novel *Don't Touch Me* was, in fact, non-fiction.

CHAPTER 9

Incorporating Psychic Abilities into Your Life

I am an American physicist, born in Chicago in 1934, and I had the great good fortune to have terrific parents and no brothers or sisters. I was very tall and skinny, which made me a very odd-looking package going to high school—six feet tall and on roller-skates. What does this have to do with being psychic? Well, we're getting there.

Being tall and thin isn't so bad, but I had, and still have, exceptionally poor vision. I still can't see what's written on a blackboard, no matter how close I sit. This is probably one of the factors that led me to study optics and lasers. My parents were well aware that even my corrected vision was close to legally blind. So there was definitely no bicycle riding on the streets of New York in my future. At least, not yet.

By 1949, I had been roller skating everywhere for a decade without any accidents. By then I was fifteen years old and a senior in high school, and the most important event taking place in my world was the devaluation of the British Pound. That meant that I could take the subway to Macy's department store and buy a brand-new, imported from England, Raleigh three-speed bicycle for fifty dollars—an amount that I could shake out of my piggy bank. I rode it home down Fifth Avenue to our apartment in Greenwich Village and brought it up in the elevator. Soon we moved to Queens, and I rode my bike several miles to Queens College every day for four years. We'll talk about the motorcycle later. My transportation tales are interesting and a little mysterious. But the story really begins in Chicago.

My mother, Anne, was a writer and a publicist. My father, William, was a book seller with a shop in downtown Chicago. Even as a child, I was aware that he had a lot of famous authors hanging out in his shop. We would hear about the latest activities of Richard Wright, James T. Farrell, Nelson Algren, Mario Puzo, and many others. Then, when my father became a New York publisher, he published books by all of them, including Puzo's *The Godfather*. My father was well known in Chicago for his deep interest in and knowledge about rare books and book collecting. In addition, he was very interested in science fiction, mysticism, and magic.

Next door to his shop was a store that sold so-called tricks and jokes. These simple mechanical magic tricks were just the thing to engage a mechanically minded eight-year-old. My first contact with a "magic" trick was a set of nested wooden boxes. These were set up so that if I could palm away your quarter, I could make it magically reappear in a little sack in the innermost box. I soon had a "magic set" that included Chinese linking rings and a deck of marked cards. What could be more fun than learning to fool adults? This would be my first contact with the idea of pretend mind reading. Eventually, I became very skillful at this using ordinary playing cards. You have all heard the magician's patter, "pick a card, any card." By the time you have gotten to this point, the magician knows

Figure 38. William Targ's Chicago rare and used bookstore:
fantasy, science fiction, and magic, 1940

what card you are going to choose, and he has a duplicate in his pocket. My favorite trick.

We moved to New York City when I was twelve years old. My junior high school was on the waterfront, on Hudson Street. During lunch break, I would sometimes take a ferry boat across the river through the ice floes to Hoboken, New Jersey. Occasionally, I missed class when we got stranded in the ice. What kid would not love that? From school, I could walk a mile down Christopher Street to my home on Fifth Avenue, but my real interest was Hubert's Flea Circus and "museum" on 42nd Street. For a quarter, I could go to the basement and watch a professional magician doing close-up magic on a stage while I stood just a few feet away. They also had a strongman who could bend railroad spikes, and an armless woman who could type with her toes. There was also a person called Albert/Alberta who manifested both male and

Figure 39. Hubert's Arcade on 42nd Street, with a magic show in the basement (1946)

female external sexual characteristics. The museum called her a hermaphrodite, but polite company today would call her mixed gender.

It was a lot for a twelve-year-old to process. For another quarter, I could participate in a shooting gallery, with rifles and real .22 caliber bullets. No, my very poor vision does not interfere with my ability to shoot at a stationary target twenty-five feet away. In fact, I used to own a magnificent Walther PPK .22 automatic pistol, which I would take to a local out-door shooting range.

But, back to 42nd Street. After the entertainment, I could then go upstairs in the same building as the magic show and visit the professional-magic retail shops, such as Holden's or D. Robbins, where they would show me tricks and allow me to buy the ones that I liked—if I could afford them. These shops, still in business, were the first places that I ever heard people talking about mental telepathy. Of course, it was all fake mind reading. But you have to start somewhere.

During this period, the great magician Blackstone came to New York, and my father was able to get us tickets close to the stage so that I could see every move the great man made. It was thrilling to see the beautiful woman vanish before my eyes in a flash of light, even though I had a pretty good idea where she went. My experience with Blackstone went far toward encouraging my interest and getting me on stage to do "fake" magic.

It was during this same period that my father published the biographies of the "notorious" Russian psychic, Helena Blavatsky, founder of the Theosophical Society, and the world-famous psychic Eileen Garrett, who was also president of the Parapsychology Foundation. Reading their books helped stimulate my interest in the paranormal field. It didn't hurt that Eileen Garrett's office was on West 57th Street, right next to my father's office and just across the street from the Russian Tea Room.

Two years after my introduction to Hubert's, I was sitting in my high school sophomore biology class when the teacher introduced us to a well-dressed and nice-looking upperclassman named Robert Rosenthal. He wanted to tell us punky fourteen-year-olds the exciting things he had learned about J. B. Rhine's ESP cards. He showed us the now-famous Zener cards showing a circle, cross, wavy lines, square, and star. He had several decks of these to pass around the classroom.

Rosenthal explained that some people were very talented at guessing these cards when they were hidden from them while being looked at by another person. We learned that this ability

Figure 40. Zener cards

was called mental telepathy. He went on to tell us that some people in Rhine's lab were even able to name the cards without having another person see them. This was called clairvoyance—a totally new word for almost everyone. We were encouraged to form little groups and to try to guess the cards that one person was looking at. You will not be surprised to learn that this was not very successful.

Nonetheless, I was totally hooked. The next Saturday, I got on the subway from Queens, where I was now living, and I went to find the American Society for Psychical Research (ASPR) on Central Park West. The ladies at the front desk were very polite and friendly toward the nearsighted string bean from Queens. They could tell that I knew a little something and was very eager to learn more. They allowed me to join the society, and they gave me several of their journals to take home. Over the next few years, I read them all. I have no doubt that it was Rosenthal and his enthusiasm that sent me on my way.

Rosenthal went on to become a very famous Harvard psychology professor. He discovered the "experimenter effect," in which the experimenter can often determine the outcome of an experiment for which he has a strongly favored belief. The most alarming demonstration of this phenomenon was called the Pygmalion Effect, in which a teacher can, by their good wishes, greatly increase the measured IQs of certain favored students.

So there I was, a fourteen-year-old who has learned that there is *real* magic. But I was still doing fake magic on the stage. It would be another twenty years before I got my hands on powerful real magic.

A good friend of our family, John Groth, had been a war correspondent and artist in WWII. In 1948, he wanted to have an art opening at a fashionable New York gallery to celebrate and sell some of his recent work in watercolors and pastels. It may sound odd, but John asked my father if I would be available to do a magic show to open his exhibit. I knew John and his wife, Ann, and was happy to open the show for him.

This was a pretty formal gathering, and each person had to purchase a ticket to gain admission and to help support John. The patrons spent about half an hour looking at John's artwork and drinking cold champagne; then I was called upon to do my half-hour magic show. I was just a kid, but I was skillful enough so that nobody was embarrassed by my performance. Then, much to my surprise, Ann called me over and said, "Our young magician will now reach into the big snifter and pull out the winning ticket for one of John's beautiful paintings." These were like old-fashioned movie tickets, each with a number printed on it. I reached in and stirred up the two hundred or so tickets. I pulled one out and handed it to Ann, the print being too small for me to read.

She looked at the ticket and read out a five or six digit number. She called out, "Does anybody have this number?" Not a sound. It occurred to me that I was given a ticket when I entered the gallery. I reached into my jacket and pulled out the ticket. As you have guessed by now, it was the winner! There was quite a hubbub over what to do. Ann said that the right thing to do was let me keep the painting that I won fair and square and have me pull out another ticket.

Again, I stirred the tickets, pulled one out, and gave it to Ann. She read the number and, after a long silence, I heard my father call out from the back of the room, "I guess he's done it again. It's my ticket." Pulling two winning tickets out of two hundred—for my own family!—is an event whose odds are 40,000 to 1 against chance. As a memory of this great synchronicity, I have the two beautiful watercolors over my desk today.

This was a wonderful event, and now, seventy-five years later, I am still thinking about synchronicity. Carl Jung and the great physicist, Wolfgang Pauli, cowrote a book about the mysterious world of acausal events—or synchronicities. This amazing book is called *The Interpretation of Nature and the Psyche.*[1] Jung saw this phenomenon in his patients, with their synchronicities and precognitive dreams. Pauli, himself, had many precognitive dreams that alerted him to the fact that ordinary causality was not always the answer, which is a big problem for physicists. He was also aware that his presence in a town where a sensitive experiment was being done was enough to almost guarantee the failure of the experiment. In psychical research, we would call this the opposite of a psi-conducive personality.

In terms of synchronicities, it required eleven coincidences in a row to allow our Star Gate program to go forward. I will

Figure 41. John Groth's painting, "GI giving candy to a Dutch girl," that Russell won

Figure 42. John Groth's painting, "Bullfight," that William Targ won

describe that later in the Star Gate section of this chapter. Another excellent book dealing with this subject is *The Roots of Coincidence*,[2] by Arthur Koestler.

By 1954, I had put Hubert's Arcade well behind me. I had graduated from Queens College having taken lots of classes in psychology and obtaining a degree in physics. My year of abnormal psychology was probably the most illuminating class and the best preparation for running a program in which I would be teaching people how to get in touch with their hidden psychic abilities.

In 1956, I left Columbia University, where I had been a moderately unsuccessful graduate student for two years. They didn't throw me out. It became clear to me, though, that Queens College had not prepared me to be a theoretical physicist, which is where Columbia had their focus. I was twenty-two years old.

This was also the year in which Morey Bernstein, who was a Colorado businessman, pursued an amateur interest in hypnotism and coaxed a young Irish woman into recounting a previous life as a woman named Bridey Murphy. Bernstein's book, *The Quest for Bridey Murphy*, was published in 1956 and became a bestseller. It was a public lecture by Bernstein that drew me to the New York Theosophical Society, to their large brownstone building on East 53rd Street.

It became clear to me that Helena Blavatsky, the society's founder in 1875, was interested in just the sorts of things that fascinated me. She once said, "The goal for the society is to further understand the mysteries of the universe and to expand the hidden capabilities of man." She and her intensely

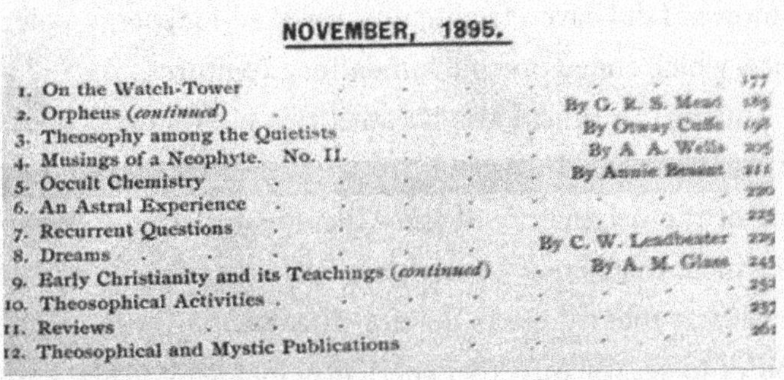

NOVEMBER, 1895.

1. On the Watch-Tower . . . 177
2. Orpheus (*continued*) . . . By G. R. S. Mead 185
3. Theosophy among the Quietists . . . By Otway Cuffe 198
4. Musings of a Neophyte. No. II. . . . By A. A. Wells 205
5. Occult Chemistry . . . By Annie Besant 211
6. An Astral Experience . . . 220
7. Recurrent Questions . . . 225
8. Dreams . . . By C. W. Leadbeater 229
9. Early Christianity and its Teachings (*continued*) . . . By A. M. Glass 245
10. Theosophical Activities . . . 252
11. Reviews . . . 257
12. Theosophical and Mystic Publications . . . 261

Figure 43. Annie Besant's first steps toward a psychic table of the elements

psychic colleagues, Annie Besant and Charles Leadbeater, were to become notably successful pioneers in applied clairvoyance. As I mentioned earlier, Annie Besant presented drawings of a psychically perceived hydrogen atom in the theosophical journal, *Lucifer,* sixty-nine years before the quark was proposed.[3]

At the Theosophical Society, I began learning how to meditate. I became interested in kundalini meditation as taught in a large illustrated volume compiled by Sir John Woodroffe (also known by his pseudonym Arthur Avalon). This book, called *The Serpent Power,* describes how to become aware of "the divine cosmic energy latent in every human being."[4] This is the "serpent" energy along your spine (along the chakras) that you can learn to "awaken." This energetic manipulation can be both pleasing and dangerous. The famous yogi mystic Gopi Krishna wrote several books describing the perils of practicing kundalini meditation without a teacher.

In addition to experiencing surprising energy, you have the opportunity to "open the crown chakra," which can give you access to the cosmos; I found this particularly interesting.

However, I did have a frightening, unasked-for energy experience, which ended my solo kundalini adventures.

During this time, I also became friends with the president of the American Theosophical Society, Dora Kunz, who was one of the originators of the "Therapeutic Touch" healing treatment that is now widely practiced by nurses. Part of her sensitivity that led her to develop Therapeutic Touch was her ability to see, or directly experience, magnetic fields. I witnessed this firsthand when she allowed me to hide little magnets in various places around her office. She was able to tell where they were hidden and describe her experience of the magnetic field.

Not long after getting to know Dora, I was scheduled to travel to England to visit a friend at Cambridge. I had a wonderful five days crossing the Atlantic on the *New Amsterdam*, a luxury liner. Nothing to do except play ping pong, play bridge, and eat.

At Cambridge, my friend Arnold Faden, an economist and visiting Fellow at Kings College, helped me find a professor who was studying just what I wanted to know. One professor was measuring how strong of a magnetic field was necessary for a person to experience visual phosphines (colored lights). It sounded interesting until I saw what he was doing. In his experiment, he used a very powerful microwave magnetron, but I didn't think that was exactly what I was looking for.

Later, Arnold found a biology laboratory where the almost blind *Gymnarchus niloticus* (African knifefish) was being studied. This fish sends out an electrical signal from its tail and can detect the radar-like return with a sensor in its head. That seemed more like what I was after. We could collect these fish with a magnet, like iron filings. The fish could detect weak magnet fields, just like Dora could. This gave me a clear example of direct perception of small magnetic fields in the animal kingdom. What I learned is that you don't have to "fry" a person with microwaves for them to be able to detect a magnetic field.

After leaving Cambridge, I located the English Theosophical Society, which had a delightful summer camp I attended in Camberley, a small town just south of London. From there I drove across the Moors to Land's End to meet an English bishop associated with the Theosophical Society, and I spent a stimulating week with him before returning to America. But now is the time to tell you that I went there, and everywhere else in England, on my brand-new motorcycle!

No, I do not have the power to cloud men's minds. It's just that in trusting England there is no vision test if all you want is a "learner's" license. There is only a written test that determines your good character. The final test question asks you if you can read a number-plate from twenty-five yards distance. Being in a strange country, in a strange crowded shop, and with very poor vision, I read the question as "twenty-five feet." I felt I would have no trouble with that, so I answered yes.

Indeed, I did not have any mishaps for my four months on the road in England. I successfully rode my 50cc Mobylette moped from Cambridge to Land's End in the south. When I returned to the United States, I was able to convince the motor-vehicle bureaucrats that I had an English driver's license in my hand, and "they don't even drive on the right side of the road." I was rewarded—not with a kick in the behind, but rather with the US driver's license that I never thought I would receive. Perhaps I *can* cloud men's minds.

Figure 44. Russell's 50cc moped (left); the 250 cc Night Hawk (right) that the "blind" biker rode for thirty-five years through Silicon Valley

That September, I returned to the US to begin my first paying job. I was going to be a microwave engineer doing research for the Sperry Gyroscope Company in Great Neck, Long Island. My boss was a very friendly PhD physicist named Morris Ettenberg, who also taught Midrash (Torah) at the Hebrew Theological Seminary on Riverside Drive, near my home. Two years of graduate school at Columbia was a pretty good job recommendation. Morris knew of my interest in psychic things, and it didn't seem to hurt our relationship. In fact, it occurred to me that Morris might have hired me, principally, to chat with him during our hour-long drive from Sperry to our homes on the Upper West Side of Manhattan.

One day, while riding home with the sun in my eyes, I told Morris that I was seeing an image. It was a white-on-black picture of a Hebrew document that had red flowers and green leaves around the edge. It was on an oval table with candles. I do not read Hebrew writing. Morris said that it sounded like his rabbi's dining room in Brooklyn.

The following day, Morris invited me to his home on Riverside Drive. He had contacted his rabbi, who had confirmed that he had such a document, and Morris had been kind enough to drive to Brooklyn to get it. The document, a photostatic copy of a Hebrew manuscript, had green checks on it for sentences that the rabbi considered correct and red circles for errors in the manuscript. Seeing the document was actually shocking for me. This was a completely unasked-for, correct hypnogogic image. Morris seemed pretty shocked also.

Back when my father had published Eileen Garrett's autobiography, I visited her at her offices on West 57th Street, and she gave me her monograph, *Mind, Matter, and Gravitation,* published by the Parapsychology Foundation. In it, she described the psychokinesis experiments of the Swedish physicist Haakon Forwald. He was investigating the ability of his subjects to deflect metal cubes as they tumbled down an incline. He found good success for several years under well-controlled conditions.

Eileen had asked me to build a similar electro-mechanical gadget for her laboratory director, Karlis Osis. I did that, and they found similar results to Forwald's using my machine and ten plastic dice that would drop down an incline onto an enclosed tabletop. (I believe that the Parapsychology Foundation still has this well-built device.)

At Sperry, I was building electron-beam microwave tubes, called "traveling wave" tubes. I had the idea that it would be easier to deflect slow electrons than metal or plastic cubes. With Morris Ettenberg's support, I built an electron beam vacuum tube with an exceptionally slow beam, which I used to demonstrate that an engineer could use his mind to move the beam to the left or right. I called this a Plasmatron. The

Figure 45. Eileen Garrett, medium and parapsychologist for half a century

results were recorded on chart paper and published in Edgar Mitchell's anthology *Psychic Exploration.*[5] One enthusiastic engineer gave a very strong signal-to-noise ratio, which is the one that I published.

In 1958, I was in the hospital with mononucleosis when my friend, Gordon Gould from Columbia, came to visit me. He understood that I was having a nice time with Morris Etten-berg and high-powered microwaves. He was starting a new company, Technical Research Group (TRG), also on Long Island, to build the world's first laser. By then, I'd had three years' experience with microwave discharge in gases, just what you need to light up a laser.

I moved over to TRG, where I had the opportunity to work on setting up one of the world's first laser labs. We did not

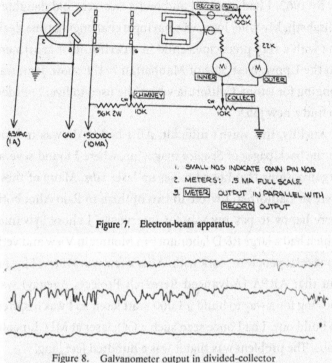

Figure 7.   Electron-beam apparatus.

1. SMALL NOS INDICATE CONN PIN NOS
2. METERS: .5 MA FULL SCALE.
3. METER OUTPUT IN PARALLEL WITH RECORD OUTPUT

Figure 8.   Galvanometer output in divided-collector electron-beam experiment.

Figure 46. Electron beam schematic; electron beam published data

make the first laser. That was built by Ted Maiman on May 16, 1960, at Hughes Research Laboratory in California. It was excited by shining a bright, flash-photography lamp on a ruby rod. But I believe that my colleague and good friend, Gerald Grosof, and I built the first laser *amplifier* (using mercury and krypton), which was instrumental in eventually getting the very valuable laser patent awarded to Gould. (Gordon had filed the first patent on the laser, but he didn't win the patent battle with Bell Labs until 1987.) I worked at TRG for three years and achieved a number of other "firsts."

By 1962, I had married and had a two-year-old daughter, Elisabeth. My wife, Joan, was having a challenging time dealing with a very precocious child in a twelfth-floor apartment on the Upper West Side of Manhattan in the snow. Joan was longing for sunny California where she used to live. I needed to find a new job.

Luckily, this wasn't difficult. All I had to do was to look in the back pages of *Science* magazine, where I found several organizations that hoped to set up laser labs. Many of these were in California. I wrote to two of them in Palo Alto; both were happy to pay my way for interviews. I chose Sylvania, which had a large R&D laboratory in Mountain View and very congenial people to work with. After a few years there, I found out that ARPA (Advanced Research Projects Agency) was looking for a way to build a 1,000-watt laser, so I was inspired to build one. I had once seen such a CO_2 laser at MIT Lincoln Labs. The problem was that it was a hundred feet long!

I had an idea for building the laser in a one-meter package. We could air-condition the laser with a big fan and an automobile heat exchanger. I worked on this machine for almost a year with two other engineers. In 1969, we topped the thousand-watt mark and had a press conference at the 21 Club in New York. We called the device the Gas Transport Laser. It was a very successful project. We sold one to General Electric for heat treating locomotive cylinders. We also sold one to Lockheed Missiles and Space Corp, where I eventually went to work.

As you can see in Figure 47, the first lasers were quite large. There is a one-meter measuring stick next to the laser to give an idea of scale. The big cylinder in the background contains

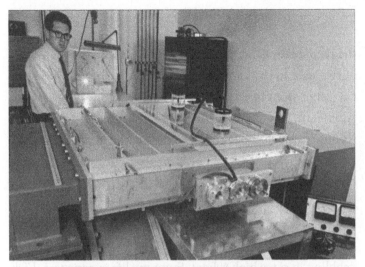

Figure 47. The 1,000-watt CO_2 laser at the Sylvania lab,
the world's highest powered one in 1969

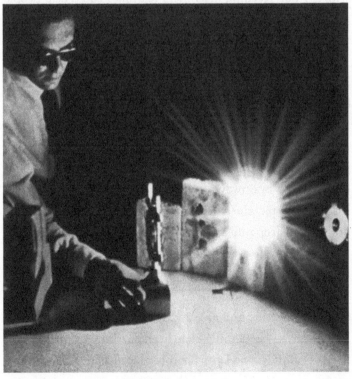

Figure 48. The laser at work

the recirculating fan. In Figure 48, I am using the full power of the laser to drill a hole in a firebrick to impress a skeptical visitor from the Army, who didn't trust our power meter. Afterward, I handed him the firebrick with a red-hot hole still shining through the entire thickness of the brick. He got the idea, and I got ultra-violet burns on my cornea similar to snow blindness. My dark glasses shielded me from the 1,000-watt laser but not the white-hot brick.

After ten years of laser research, I started seriously looking for a way to enter parapsychology research, which I had been dabbling in since high school. From my life experiences, I felt confident that psychic abilities are natural. From my experience with my ESP teaching machine, I felt that I could help people get in touch with their own psychic abilities. I was willing to risk my very successful laser career to attempt that endeavor.

In April 1972, I went to the CIA to talk with Dr. Kit Green, head of the Life Science Division. He was somewhat interested because he was already supporting my friend Andrija Puharich by providing him with Eastern Bloc ESP data. But nothing substantive happened at my meeting. At the same time, my good friend Jean Millay was giving a workshop showing her bio-feedback brainwave-synchronizing device at the Esalen Institute. People who can synchronize (phase lock) their alpha brainwaves drop into a strong and surprising empathetic and loving state. She was studying synchronization, but I was about to experience a whole string of synchronicities.

Jean invited me to come to Esalen to demonstrate my ESP teaching machine and give a talk on Russian and American ESP research—something I had been pursuing since I had met Sheila Ostrander and Lynn Schroeder at my father's seventieth birthday party. They had written *Psychic Discoveries behind the Iron Curtain*,[6] and I'd had an opportunity to chat with them about it.

I went with Jean, gave my talk, and met the Esalen owner and manager Mike Murphy. The next day, I got a call from my new friend Mike. He was scheduled to give a similar presentation on US and Soviet ESP research at Grace Cathedral in San Francisco. However, he had become ill, and he couldn't keep his date. Could I go to San Francisco the next day and give the same talk I had just given at Esalen? How likely is that?

Of course I said yes. After my lecture, a man named Art Reetz came up to me. He was the "New Projects Administrator" at NASA and was organizing a conference on "Speculative Technology" in May on St. Simons Island, off the coast of Georgia. It just so happened that he was strolling down the street past Grace Cathedral that day and saw that someone was lecturing on US and Soviet ESP research. He had liked my talk, he said. Would I be interested in coming to his conference to present it again? Being a physicist, I would be welcome. Yes, I would be happy to attend this fancy new technology conference. How likely is that?

The next day, in the Palo Alto newspaper, I read that Hal Puthoff, an SRI laser researcher, was giving a talk on US and Soviet ESP research at Stanford. I attended Hal's lecture. He knew of me from my laser work. I told him about my NASA conference and asked him, if I were able to get NASA money, if he would support my joining him at SRI to start an ESP research program. He said yes.

At the St. Simons conference, I struck up a conversation with pioneering space engineer Wernher von Braun. He told me about his amazingly psychic grandmother, and he was pleased when he scored excellently on my ESP teaching machine, which I had brought to the conference. He rang the little bell time after time. This is very unlikely.

I told von Braun that I was seeking NASA support for my gadget "to teach NASA astronauts to become sensitive to their spacecraft, so they could anticipate accidents." He thought that was a great idea and took me to meet the NASA chief administrator, James Fletcher. Von Braun was probably remembering the near-disaster of *Apollo 13* almost two years earlier, when an oxygen tank exploded due to an overheated power switch.

Fletcher also thought I had a good idea and agreed with von Braun that NASA could give me $80,000, *if I could do the project at SRI.* Yes!

At that very moment, astronaut Edgar Mitchell walked by and told us that he was working with Willis Harman at SRI to start his own project, the Institute of Noetic Sciences, and he would be happy to help us.

The next week, Hal, Mitchell, Harman, and I met with the president of SRI, Charley Anderson, in his office. We made an agreement to take NASA's money and start the program at SRI in September, after I came back from Iceland, where I was watching my brother-in-law Bobby Fischer in the 1972 World Chess Championship (he won!). And that is how the SRI Star Gate program got started, coincidence after coincidence.

In 1982, I left SRI and organized Delphi Associates with two other partners, Keith Harary and Anthony White. Tony White was a successful businessman and investor. Keith was a very gifted psychic and psychologist who had been with the SRI

Figure 49. Wernher von Braun at NASA conference on Speculative Technology (1972)

Figure 50. Early ESP trainer that von Braun used at the conference

Figure 51. Three great stars of the Star Gate program:
Pat Price (the psychic policeman), Hella Hammid (control and highest
scoring subject), and Ingo Swann (the psychic father of remote viewing)

program for several years as a researcher and remote viewer. Delphi, a company born entirely out of our imagination, had two large psi projects and a number of small ones during its three-year life.

For our first project, our team of psychics and investors wanted to investigate the possibility of using psychic abilities to make money in the marketplace. The second big project was a three-year effort in which we designed psychic video games for Atari—the Silicon Valley game company. (By the way, we were one of the few consultants to actually get paid, as Atari imploded from $2 billion to zero in the fall of 1995.)

For our market-forecasting project, we were very fortunate to add to our merry band a spiritually minded and enthusiastic big-time investor, Paul Temple, and a highly intelligent and adventurous stockbroker, John Rende. It is well understood that reading numbers or letters psychically is an exceptionally difficult task, so we knew we couldn't forecast silver commodity prices by asking our psychic to read the symbols that would appear the following week on the Big Board at the Commodity Exchange.

Instead, we used a symbolic protocol first described by Stephan Schwartz of the Mobius Society. He describes this in his book, *Opening to the Infinite.*[7] In this scheme, we associated a different object with each of the possible states (prices) the market could produce the following week. We wanted to know a week in advance if the commodity called "December Silver" (which can be purchased any time before December) would be "up a little" (less than a quarter), "up a lot" (more than a quarter), "down a little or unchanged," or "down a lot." These are four discrete conditions that could be represented by or associated with four objects; for example, a light bulb, a flower, a book, and a stuffed animal.

For one week's trial, we would ask our businessman, Tony White—who actually ran the project because of secrecy requirements from Keith and me (viewer and interviewer)—to choose four such strongly differing objects (orthogonal targets) each week and associate one of them with each of our four possible market conditions.

Only Tony knew the objects. And, of course, no one knew the correct object. I would then interview the remote viewer, Keith, over the telephone on Monday and ask him to describe his impressions of the object we would show him *on Friday*. The broker would then buy or sell silver futures based entirely on what the viewer saw, whether it be a flower, a teddy bear, or whatever. That would be the object associated with what the market would do over the next four days, which is why this protocol was called "associative" remote viewing (ARV). At

Figure 52. Front page *Wall Street Journal* article

the end of the week, when silver finally closed, we would give
the viewer feedback by showing him the object corresponding
to what the market *actually did*.

Of our nine forecasts in the fall of 1982, all nine were correct, but the broker declined to take our advice on two of them.
We earned $240,000, which we divided evenly between Delphi
and our investor. (In 1982, $240,000 was a lot of money.) In
fact, our enterprise was on the front page of the *Wall Street
Journal*. Erik Larson wrote the article, "Did Psychic Powers
Give Firm a Killing in the Silver Market?"[8]

In 1983, television producer Tony Edwards made a film
about us for BBC's *Horizon*. It later became a PBS *NOVA*

program called "The Case of ESP." This was first aired in England as a ninety-minute program on BBC, then later as a fifty-five-minute program in the US. WGBH Boston explained to me that they had to edit out the live and successful remote viewing session from the original BBC version because US audiences have a much shorter attention span than English viewers.

"The Case of ESP" was frequently shown on PBS from 1984 until 1995, at which time, for some unknown reason, it disappeared from *NOVA's* archives. It is now also gone from the archives of WGBH, Boston, who produced the film, and from *Time-Life Books*, who distributed it for sale. Its existence is not a fantasy since I have several tapes and DVD copies of the original program on my desk. Interestingly, 1995 was also the year in which the remote viewing program was officially declassified and terminated by the CIA. The disappearance of the film has never been explained. My guess is that the CIA put pressure on *NOVA* to pull the film, since *NOVA* alone was the US copyright holder, and only they could have accomplished such a complete erasure.

Full disclosure—in the following year, we were not successful in our silver forecasting; possibly because our investor wanted to accelerate the trial rate to twice a week. With that protocol, the viewer did not receive timely feedback from the previous trial. My personal belief is that we lost our spiritual and scientific focus and became overcome by the thought of limitless wealth. Though different people had different opinions on the reasons for our failure to replicate the success, we all became very tired of people telling us that it must have been our lucky day.

The good news is that silver forecasting was once again successful in 1996. I worked with my friend and writing partner, Jane Katra, a spiritual healer with a PhD in health education, and with two other good friends who were mathematicians— Dean and Wendy Brown. In a very friendly and open emotional environment, we used a redundancy coding protocol and obtained eleven hits in twelve trials for silver futures—a result significant at odds of 3 in 1,000.

Every week, Jane and I each had our own unique target pool. The idea of *redundancy coding* is that we must have *agreement* on the forecast direction of the market by Jane and me (for silver to go up or down) for the trial to go forward—even though the objects in our individual target pools were entirely different. This highly significant result shows the efficacy of redundancy coding even when the psychics are amateurs. We published our results, even though no money was involved.[9]

Since I left SRI about forty years ago, I have been traveling all over the world teaching people how to do remote viewing. I was invited four years in a row to an Italian astrological group. Every year, there were forty very enthusiastic women, who didn't know anything about remote viewing or what I would be having them do. At the end of a weeklong class, I would do a double-blind trial in which each person would get four hidden pictures, one at a time, to try to match with one of four other pictures, each in its own envelope. After each woman had described and drawn her psychic impressions of a hidden photo, I would ask her to decide which of the four photos in the envelopes best matched her drawing. This would be

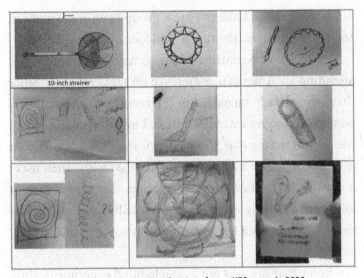

Figure 53. Psychic strainer drawings from a UFO group in 2020

repeated for each of the four pictures. Some would even dowse over the envelopes to try to get a better "reading."

Basically, you would expect a person to get one out of four correct just by chance. Members of my groups all averaged two to three out of four. This is two to three times chance expectation. With a class of forty, this would verge on odds of 1 in 1,000, year after year. After my fourth year, I described these results to the final large group meeting.

I asked them to tell me why the Italian women did so much better than American women. One woman, who was sitting up front in a smart black dress said, "Everybody knows that Italian woman are the most beautiful and the most sexy. Why shouldn't they also be the most psychic?" I think that this says something about their self-esteem. The only Americans who did as well as the Italians were a group from the American Society of Dowsers. They are psychic for a living.

The people who contributed the pictures in Figure 53 were attending an American conference on UFO research. Since they were already interested in "extranormal" phenomena, I was invited to give a demonstration. I told the audience that I had an interesting object in my briefcase. I said, "Quiet your mind by whatever means you are familiar with. Then make a drawing of the first surprising images that appear in your awareness." This is what I have been telling people for fifty years, whether it's a top government bureaucrat or a visiting psychic.

I know that this was not a double-blind experiment, since I knew what the object was, but I am very experienced at saying nothing. This group of UFO watchers did exceedingly well with my difficult target. It was a very large, wire spaghetti strainer. The target is at the top left of the illustration, followed by a sampling of the drawings.

Padmasambhava

Figure 54. Padmasambhava, 800 AD,
"Our nature is timeless awareness, free of cause and effect."

In approximately 800 AD, Padmasambhava, who was known as a great dharma master in India, was invited by the king of Tibet to come to his country to bring an end to internecine religious wars. He taught Dzogchen Buddhism, which is not a religion but rather "the primordial state of the individual, the nature of the mind itself is like a mirror which has the natural capacity to reflect whatever is set before it. It is the same with the nature of contemplation. There is nothing to correct or modify. What the practitioner does when entering contemplations is simply to discover himself in the condition of the mirror."[1] This is the teaching of his widely read meditation book, *Self-Liberation through Seeing with Naked Awareness*.

Padmasambhava was a Hindu, as was the Buddha. The great master who followed them in the 14th century was Longchen Robjam, known as Longchenpa. His Precious Treasury series of books is considered the pinnacle of Dzogchen writing. They contain no deities, and they urge the practitioner to reside in timeless awareness and spaciousness and to experience liberation and freedom, since that is our true nature. This is the natural home for a remote viewer, and there is no better teacher than Longchenpa. The easiest of his books to read is *The Precious Treasury of the Basic Space of Phenomena*. This book is a true *transmission* of the teaching directly into the heart of the reader.

A long time before Padmasambhava, in 200 BC, an Indian Hindu teacher, Patanjali, told us that if we can reach the meditative state of Samadhi, then we will be able to see into the distance and into the future. From that place, we will be able to diagnose the sick and heal all illness. Though he tells us a lot about that state, he doesn't really tell us how to get there. I believe that Padmasambhava gives directions on how to achieve timeless awareness, through practice—or at least that's his intention.

For the remote viewer, this valuable teaching is that we should notice that our nature is "timeless awareness," not meat and potatoes. Since your nature is timeless awareness, you are *free in your meditation to move your awareness anywhere you wish through space and time without limitation.* Since your awareness is timeless, you are free of the limitations of cause and effect. This is why all our data show that the awareness of the remote viewer permeates everything.

It is within that context that the interviewer instructs the remote viewer, "Just tell us what you are experiencing. Don't try to change anything." I hope that you can make use of the techniques described in this book, that you have learned a little something from the masters, and that you, too, can do as they do.

NOTES

CHAPTER 1

1. Ingo Swann and Nick Cook, *Resurrecting the Mysterious: Ingo Swann's "Great Lost Work"* (n.p.: BioMind Superpowers Books, 2020), 151.

2. Edwin May and Sonali Marwaha, *The Star Gate Archives: Reports of the United States Government Sponsored Psi Program, 1972-1995. Volume 1: Remote Viewing, 1972-1984* (Jefferson, NC: McFarland & Co., 2018), 71.

CHAPTER 2

1. Stephen M. Phillips, "Extrasensory Perception of Subatomic Particles," *Journal of Scientific Exploration* 9, no. 4 (1995): 489.

CHAPTER 3

1. Russell Targ and Harold E. Puthoff, "Information Transmission under Conditions of Sensory Shielding," *Nature* 252 (Oct. 1974): 602–607.

CHAPTER 4

1. Harold E. Puthoff and Russell Targ, "A Perceptual Channel for Information Transfer over Kilometer Distances: Historical Perspective and Recent Research," *Proc. IEEE* 64, no. 3 (March 1976): 329–254.

CHAPTER 7

1. Ludwig Wittgenstein, *Tractatus Logico-Philosophicus* (London: Routledge & Kegan Paul, 1922).

2. Upton Sinclair, *Mental Radio* (self-published, 1930; Charlottesville, VA: Hampton Roads, 2000). Citations refer to the Hampton Roads edition.

3. William Cox, "Precognition: An Analysis," *J. ASPR* 50 (1956): 99–109.

4. Erwin Schrödinger, "Discussion of Probability Relations between Separated Systems," *Proceedings of the Cambridge Philosophical Society* 31 (1936): 555.

5. Lee Billings, "Explorers of Quantum Entanglement Win 2022 Nobel Prize in Physics," *Scientific American* (October 2022).

6. Gertrude Schmeidler, "An Experiment in Precognitive Clairvoyance: Part-1. The Main Results" and "Part-2. The Reliability of the Scores," *Journal of Parapsychology* 28 (1964): 1–27.

7. Charles Honorton and Diane Ferari, "Future-Telling: A Meta-Analysis of Forced-Choice Precognition Experiments," *Journal of Parapsychology* 53 (December 1989): 281–209.

8. Dean Radin, *The Conscious Universe* (San Francisco: Harper Edge, 1997).

9. William Braud, *Distant Mental Influence* (Charlottesville, VA: Hampton Roads, 2003).

10. Zoltán Vassy, "Method for Measuring the Probability of 1 Bit Extrasensory Information Transfer between Living Organisms," *Journal of Parapsychology* 42 (1978): 158–160.

11. Deryl Bem, "Feeling the Future: Anomalous Retroactive Influences on Cognition and Affect," *Journal of Personality and Social Psychology* (December 2010).

CHAPTER 8

1. H. E. Puthoff, "Feasibility Study on the Vulnerability of the MPS System to RV Detection Techniques," SRI Internal Report (15 April 1979; revised 2 May 1979).

2. Joe McMoneagle, *Remote Viewing Secrets* (Charlottesville, VA: Hampton Roads, 2002).

3. Ingo Swann, *Natural ESP* (New York: Bantam Books, 1987).

4. René Warcollier, *Mind to Mind* (New York: Creative Edge Press, 1948; Charlottesville, VA: Hampton Roads, 2001), 5 (my italics). Citations refer to the Hampton Roads edition.

5. Upton Sinclair, *Mental Radio* (Charlottesville, VA: Hampton Roads, 2002).

6. Ibid., 104–105

7. Ibid., xi.

8. Robert Monroe, *Journeys Out of the Body* (Garden City, NY: Anchor Press, 1973).

9. Namkhai Norbu, *Dream Yoga and the Practice of Natural Light* (Ithaca, NY: Snow Lion Publications, 1992).

10. Ingo Swann, *Psychic Sexuality* (Rapid City, SD: Ingo Swann Books, 1999).

11. Aleister Crowley, *The Confessions of Aleister Crowley* (London: Penguin Books, 1979).

12. Sylvan Muldoon and Hereward Carrington, *The Projection of the Astral Body* (London: Rider & Paternoster House, 1929).

13. McKinley Kantor, *Don't Touch Me* (New York: Random House, 1951).

CHAPTER 9

1. C. G. Jung and W. Pauli, *The Interpretation of Nature and the Psyche* (London: Routledge & Kegan Paul, 1955).

2. Arthur Koestler, *The Roots of Coincidence* (New York: Vintage, 1973).

3. Annie Besant, "Occult Chemistry," *Lucifer* (November 1895): 211.

4. Sir John Woodroffe, *The Serpent Power* (Madras, India: Ganesh & Co., 1928).

5. Edgar Mitchell, *Psychic Exploration* (New York: Cosimo Books, 1974).

6. Sheila Ostrander and Lynn Schroeder, *Psychic Discoveries behind the Iron Curtain* (Hoboken, NJ: Prentice-Hall, 1970).

7. Stephan A. Schwartz, *Opening to the Infinite* (Buda, TX: Nemoseen Media, 2007).

8. Erik Larson, "Did Psychic Powers Give Firm a Killing in the Silver Market?" *Wall Street Journal* (Oct. 22, 1984).

9. Russell Targ, Jane Katra, Dean Brown, and Wendy Wiegand, "Viewing the Future: A Pilot Study with an Error-Detecting Protocol," *Journal of Scientific Exploration* 9, no. 3 (1995): 367–380.

APPENDIX

1. Padmasambhava, *Self-Liberation through Seeing with Naked Awareness* (Barrytown, NY: Station Hill Press, 1989).

INDEX

A

aesthetic sensing, 85
African jungle bomber crash, 43–44
African knifefish, 110–111
Altamonte windmill farm, 47, 48
American Society for Psychical Research (ASPR), 104
American Society of Dowsers, 127–128
American Theosophical Society, 110
  see also Theosophical Society
analytic noise, 2, 89–90
analytical cognitive style, 38
analytical overlay (AOL), 2
Anderson, Charley, 120
anticipatory reaction experiments, 72–75
Apollo 13 mission, 120
archeology applications, 32–33
architect in Italy (remote viewer), 88
ARPA (Advanced Research Projects Agency), 116

art show prize draws, 105–106, 107
Associative Remote Viewing (ARV), 79, 123–124
astrological group conference, 126–128
Atari (game company), 122
atomic bomb test viewing, 3
atomic particle visualization, 14–15, 17–18
Aviation Week articles, 25
avoidance experiments, 77–78
awareness
  limitlessness of, xx–xxi
  nonlocal, 57–58
  timeless, 3, 130–131

B

BBC *Horizon* program, 124–125
Bem, Daryl, 75–78
Bernstein, Morey, *The Quest for Bridey Murphy*, 108
Besant, Annie, 13, 14–17, 109
Bevatron, 36
Bierman, Dick, 73
Blackstone (magician), 103

ABOUT THE AUTHOR

Russell Targ is a physicist and author and was a pioneer in the development of the laser and laser applications. He holds his BS in physics from Queens College and did graduate work in physics at Columbia University. Targ has received two National Aeronautics and Space Administration awards for inventions and contributions in lasers and laser communications, and he has published over one hundred scientific papers on lasers, plasma physics, and ESP research.

In the 1970s and 1980s, Targ cofounded and worked for the CIA-sponsored Stanford Research Institute's investigation into psychic abilities. His work in this new area, called remote viewing, was published in *Nature*, the *Proceedings of the Institute of Electrical and Electronics Engineers*, and *Proceedings of the American Association for the Advancement of Science*. Targ retired from Lockheed Martin Missiles & Space Co. as a senior staff scientist, where he developed airborne laser systems for the detection of windshear.

He was most recently featured in the popular documentary *Third Eye Spies* by award-winning director Lance Mungia. It chronicles the lifelong journey of Targ's research into ESP. Targ authored *The Reality of ESP, Limitless Mind,* and *Do You*

See What I See? Memoirs of a Blind Biker. He is co-author of *Mind-Reach, The Mind Race, Miracles of Mind, The Heart of the Mind,* and *The End of Suffering.*

He lives in Palo Alto, California, with his wife Patricia. His website is *espresearch.com.*